DOMESTIC VIOLENCE

Other Books in the At Issue Series:

Affirmative Action
Business Ethics
Environmental Justice
Ethnic Conflict
Immigration Policy
Legalizing Drugs
The Media and Politics
Policing the Police
Rape on Campus
Smoking
U.S. Policy Toward China
What Is Sexual Harassment?

DOMESTIC VIOLENCE

David Bender, *Publisher*
Bruno Leone, *Executive Editor*

Scott Barbour, *Managing Editor*
Brenda Stalcup, *Series Editor*

Karin L. Swisher, *Book Editor*

An Opposing Viewpoints ® Series

Greenhaven Press, Inc.
San Diego, California

Library of Congress Cataloging-in-Publication Data

Domestic violence / Karin L. Swisher, book editor.
     p.   cm. — (At issue) (An opposing viewpoints series)
    Includes bibliographical references and index.
    ISBN 1-56510-381-5 (alk. paper). — ISBN 1-56510-380-7 (pbk. : alk. paper).
    1. Family violence. 2. Victims of family violence. I. Swisher, Karin, 1966- . II. Series. III. Series: Opposing viewpoints series (Unnumbered)
HQ809.D65 1996
362.82′92—dc20   95-24176
                                                        CIP

Table of Contents

Page

Introduction 7

1. The Problem of Domestic Violence Is Widespread 10
   R. Barri Flowers

2. Domestic Violence Is a Serious Problem for Women 22
   Erica Goode et al.

3. Domestic Violence Is a Serious Problem for Professional 28
   Women
   Hillary Johnson

4. Domestic Violence Is a Serious Problem for Black Women 37
   Shawn Sullivan

5. The Justice System Should Take Domestic Violence More 41
   Seriously
   Ann Jones

6. Domestic Violence Is a Problem for Men 50
   Murray A. Straus

7. Domestic Violence Harms Both Men and Women 65
   Tish Durkin

8. The Problem of Domestic Violence Is Exaggerated 71
   Cathy Young

9. Women Are Responsible for Domestic Violence 76
   Katherine Dunn

10. The Media Misreport Domestic Violence 80
    John Leo

11. Men and Women Both Cause Domestic Violence 83
    Judith Sherven and James Sniechowski

12. The Problem of Domestic Violence for Men Is Exaggerated 86
    Ellis Cose

Organizations to Contact 89

Bibliography 92

Index 94

Introduction

"Despite its prevalence, domestic abuse remains a gravely undercovered story. When it is covered, it is often treated as a bizarre spectacle rather than an all-too-common social crisis." This critique of the media's coverage of domestic violence was offered in 1992 by Fairness & Accuracy in Reporting, a liberal media watchdog organization. Just two years later, with the murder of Nicole Brown, the ex-wife of actor and former football star O.J. Simpson, the media would focus squarely on, and engage in an unprecedented and lengthy dialogue about, the issue of domestic violence.

Nicole Brown and her friend Ronald Goldman were stabbed to death at Brown's home on June 12, 1994. Days later, Simpson was arrested for the murders. Within weeks of the arrest, the American public learned that while married to Simpson, Brown had called the police eight times to report domestic violence. In one such incident, on January 1, 1989, she charged that Simpson had threatened to kill her; Simpson was arrested, sentenced to two years' probation, fined, and ordered to perform community service and seek counseling. Brown eventually filed for divorce in 1992.

Some experts argue that Brown's and Simpson's relationship conformed to a typical pattern of domestic violence. According to Murray A. Straus, the director of the Center on Family Violence at the University of New Hampshire, "When an assault by a husband occurs, it is not usually an isolated instance. In fact, it tends to be a recurrent feature of the relationship." Apparently Simpson abused Brown throughout their marriage, a behavior that would be consistent with this scenario. That Simpson may have killed Brown two years after the divorce also fits the experts' pattern. Some commentators argue that abused women, whether they are divorced or not, are in more danger after they leave their abusers than while living with them. Lee Rosen, chair of the American Bar Association's Domestic-Violence Council and a Raleigh, North Carolina, divorce lawyer, observes, "Seventy-five percent of the women killed by their mates are tracked down *after* they've left home."

The Simpson case has provided the impetus for public debate on the issue of domestic violence—some spectacular, some thoughtful. Many sociologists, feminists, media commentators, and advocates for policies to combat domestic violence against women argue that domestic violence is a serious social problem that deserves public attention. Others, however, have raised questions about the true seriousness of the problem and about the way the debate has been framed.

The sociologists, feminists, and others who argue that domestic violence is a serious problem contend that between two and four million women are victims each year. The authors of *No Safe Haven: Male Violence*

Against Women at Home, at Work, and in the Community assert, "Based on the last 17 years of empirical inquiry, experts now estimate that as many as *4 million women experience severe or life-threatening assault from a male partner in an average 12-month period in the United States;* and that *one in every three women* will experience at least one physical assault by an intimate partner during adulthood." In 1992, the U.S. surgeon general ranked abuse by husbands and partners as the leading cause of injury to women aged fifteen to forty-four. These advocates also argue that abuse cuts across all racial and socioeconomic lines. Although many sociologists maintain that less educated, unemployed, poor young women are more likely than others to be in abusive relationships, psychologist Robert Geffner, president of the Family Violence and Sexual Assault Institute in Tyler, Texas, says, "I'm treating physicians, attorneys, a judge, and professors who are, or were, battered women. Intelligent people let this happen, too."

Others are unconvinced that domestic violence against women is as serious a problem as some advocates have alleged. Their arguments take two forms. First, they contend that women's advocates exaggerate statistics on the number of women who suffer from domestic violence each year. The real number of abused women, these critics assert, is significantly lower than many feminists have claimed. Longtime *U.S. News & World Report* columnist John Leo says of domestic violence, "No other current topic seems so steeped in myths, bad stats, and general misinformation." As an example of legitimate research, he points to Murray A. Straus's study that shows that 1.8 million women suffer some kind of abuse each year (a figure significantly lower than many advocates' estimates) and that only 10 percent of abused women require medical attention. According to Leo, "Many studies show that the real numbers are low. . . . Numbers fed to the media are . . . routinely exaggerated and massaged into an 'epidemic' of violence."

Other commentators concur in Leo's assessment; many of them cite an FBI study done in the early 1990s that shows a drop of 18 percent since the late 1970s in the number of women killed by husbands or boyfriends each year. These commentators contend that while domestic violence is certainly a legitimate concern, many of the claims and much of the inflammatory rhetoric surrounding the claims are more likely to alienate the public than to enlist their support to find solutions.

Critics' second objection to the argument that domestic violence is a widespread problem for women focuses on the way the debate has been framed. They contend that women's abuse of men has been virtually ignored and that, by overlooking abused men, advocates are neglecting half the problem. Murray A. Straus cites research "that shows that women initiate and carry out physical assaults on their partners as often as men do." Straus concludes that while approximately 1.8 million women are assaulted each year by their husbands, an estimated 2 million men are assaulted by their wives. Psychologist Judith Sherven and behaviorist James Sniechowski agree that women are as responsible as men for domestic violence. They assert, "Domestic violence is not an either-or phenomenon. It is not either the man's fault or the woman's. It is a both-and problem." Advocates would have more success alleviating the problem, many argue, if they acknowledged women's role in perpetuating domestic violence.

Women's advocates reject the argument that domestic violence against men is as serious as that against women. They concede that men who are abused deserve sympathy and aid, but they maintain that it is women who are most often—and most violently—abused. Researchers Rebecca Dobash and Russell Dobash in *Violence Against Husbands* calculate that men are violent sixty-six times as often as women. And the Justice Department's National Crime Victimization Survey of 1973 to 1992 shows that women are about three times as likely as men to be victims of domestic violence. According to the survey, a woman is abused every fifteen seconds and four women are killed each day by their intimate male partners. Thus, these commentators argue, it would be inaccurate to inflate the seriousness of domestic violence against men to make it appear as though it occurred as often or was as detrimental as violence against women.

Commentators, sociologists, and advocates do agree that domestic violence is damaging, no matter who perpetrates it. Malcolm George, a neurophysiologist at Queen Mary and Westfield College of the University of London, notes, "Goodness and badness don't come from sex. We need to focus on real victims, irrespective of gender." The authors in *At Issue: Domestic Violence* debate the extent and nature of domestic violence and how it can be reduced.

1

The Problem of Domestic Violence Is Widespread

R. Barri Flowers

R. Barri Flowers is a criminologist and social scientist in Lake Oswego, Oregon, and the author of The Victimization and Exploitation of Women and Children, *from which this viewpoint was taken.*

Domestic violence has a long history. Social systems dating back for centuries have condoned and even encouraged men's violence toward their mates. Modern societies are no exception. Men continue to abuse the women with whom they are intimate in epidemic proportions. Sometimes the abuse is psychological, sometimes it is physical, but it is always devastating to the battered woman.

Perhaps the classic symbolization of the victimization of women is the battered woman. Not only have women been the victims of abusive husbands or boyfriends throughout history, but this form of victimization and domestic violence continues to be amongst the most hidden and painfully prevalent issues of our time. A recent study of domestic violence found women to be victims of intimates at a rate three times as often as men.[1] In this viewpoint, we will examine the problem of battered women and its implications for women and our society.

A dark history of wife abuse

Wife battering has been in existence since ancient times, often thought of as an acceptable and even expected practice. Historical literature is replete with examples of the cruelties inflicted upon women by their spouses. One article recounts the "scalding death of Fausta ordered by her husband, the Emperor Constantine, which was to serve as a precedent for the next fourteen centuries."[2]

Friedrich Engels postulated that wife abuse began "with the emergence of the first monogamous pairing relationship which replaced group marriage and the extended family of early promiscuous societies."[3] Another theory advanced that the historical condoning of violence against women is rooted in the "subjugation and oppression of women through the male partner exercising his authority as head of the family."[4]

In western society, wife battering has flourished since the Middle Ages. The rampant violence towards wives in Europe came to America with the colonists. "During one period, a husband was permitted by law to beat his wife so long as his weaponry was not bigger than his thumb."[5] Such laws remained on the books until the end of the nineteenth century.

Defining the battered woman today

For many, a battered woman continues to reflect physical abuse of some nature. One study defined battered women as

> adult women who were intentionally physically abused in ways that caused pain or injury, or who were forced into involuntary action or restrained by force from voluntary action by adult men with whom they have or had established relationships, usually involving sexual intimacy.[6]

With advances in understanding relationships and the effects of behavior, the definition of the battered woman has broadened in recent years. The term now reflects not only physical abuse of women such as beatings with fists or other objects, choking, whipping, but also psychological or emotional abuse, including threats, insults, intimidation and degradation. The perpetrators of battering include not only husbands, ex-husbands, or lovers, but children and grandchildren as well.[7]

Referring to battered women has also taken on many now common phrases such as "the battered wife or woman syndrome," "wife abuse," "woman battering," and "conjugal violence." Most important is the recognition that women can be victimized by their mates in many ways, each of which can be devastating to the woman's physical and emotional well being.

How widespread is the problem?

While most experts agree that the battering of women has reached epidemic proportions, researchers have found that women actually reporting this occurrence is far less frequent. A recent study estimated that only 1 out of every 270 incidents of wife abuse is ever reported to law enforcement.[8] In a study of women victims of battering, Denver psychologist Lenore Walker, who has done extensive research on the subject and authored several books on family violence, indicated that less than 10 percent ever reported serious violence to the police. The severe underreporting of domestically violated women can generally be attributed to the following reasons:

- Victim denial.
- Protection of the batterer.
- Disavowal techniques to keep it in the family.
- Silent desire to be abused.
- Fear of alternatives (i.e., continued abuse, loss of support).
- Shame.

Despite the cloak of silence that greatly hampers efforts at discovering and assisting battered women, researchers have found the problem to be staggering. Over a five-year period (1987–1991), the *National Crime*

Victimization Survey found that 2.9 million women were the victims of violence by intimates, for an average of 572,032 victimizations per year.[9] Diana Russell, a professor of sociology and author of *Rape in Marriage*, recently completed a survey of sexual assault of San Francisco women. Twenty-one percent of the respondents who had ever been married reported being physically abused by a husband at some stage in their lives.[10] According to a National Family Violence Survey conducted by sociologists Murray Straus and Richard Gelles, in 1985 1.7 million women were seriously physically abused by husbands or partners.[11]

Estimates of battered women have soared as high as 1 woman out of every 2. Social scientists contend that every year as many as 2 million women in the United States are beaten by their spouses.[12] According to FBI statistics, woman battering is one of the most frequently occurring crimes in the nation, with a beating taking place every 18 seconds.[13] In 1992, 29 percent of the women murdered in the United States were killed by husbands or boyfriends.[14]

Who is the battered woman?

The popular myth is that battered women are of the lower class, undereducated, and minority segments of our population. However, these groups are overrepresented in the statistics because of their greater dependency (and therefore visibility) on society's institutions for their basic survival needs.

Recent studies indicate that as many as 80 percent of the cases of battering have gone undiagnosed because of the more privileged environment in which they occur.[15] Women of every age, race, ethnicity, and social class are being battered by their husbands and lovers. What these women have in common is a low self-esteem that is usually related to repeated victimization. For some victims, this characteristic is limited only to their relationship with men; for others, low self-esteem pervades their entire existence.

Battered women typically view themselves and all women as inferior to men, have a tendency to cope with anger through denial or turning it inward, and suffer from depression, psychosomatic illnesses, and feelings of guilt. According to Terry Davidson, author of *Conjugal Crime: Understanding and Changing the Wife Beating Pattern*, victims of spousal abuse "may exemplify society's old image of ideal womanhood—submissive, religious, nonassertive, accepting of whatever the husband's life brings. . . . The husband comes first for these women, who perceive themselves as having little control over many areas of their own lives."[16]

Who are the batterers of women?

Just as the victim of battering can be any woman, the perpetrator can also be any man. Certain patterns have emerged in the character of an abusive mate. The male batterer is typically seen as possessing a dual personality. He can be either especially charming or extremely cruel. Selfishness and generosity are easily interchangeable parts of his personality, depending upon his mood. Jealousy and possessiveness are considered integral proponents in his violent disposition. The batterer's greatest fear is that the woman will leave him.

Based on a study conducted over a four-year period at New York's Abused Women's Aid in Crisis, Maria Roy, the founder and director of the organization which offers help to battered women, characterized the typical abusive male as:

- Between 26 and 35 years of age; followed by the 36 to 50 age group.
- Having a history of childhood abuse or an abusive family.
- Ninety percent do not have a criminal record, indicating that most offenders are not deviant outside of the family.

Roy further found that:

- Most abuse occurs during the first 15 years of the relationship.
- Most battering begins almost immediately after the partnership develops.
- Most abuse is physical, without the use of weapons.
- Major changes in the family life (such as loss of income and death) increase the propensity or level of violence in relationships of long duration.[17]

Symptoms of battering

Why do men physically abuse their spouses and lovers? What are the signs that abuse may be taking place? Research has shown that for many abusers sexual issues in the relationship are often symptomatic of the abuse.

Marital Rape Rape is still often thought of in terms of strangers or casual acquaintances rather than committed by lovers or husbands. Indeed, up until the mid-1970s, in most states it was not a crime for a man to rape his wife. In 1975, South Dakota became the first state to make spousal rape a crime.

Just how many men rape their wives is impossible to establish since, for many victims, this continues to be a private matter which goes unreported and unprosecuted. There is some indication that the numbers may be high. Of completed rapes reported to the *National Crime Survey* for the years 1979 to 1987, 52 percent of the rapists were intimates.[18] Studies show that 1 in 10 wives has been sexually assaulted at least once by her spouse.[19]

There is a strong correlation between marital rape and battering. Lenore Walker found that 59 percent of her sample of battered women were forced to have sex with their spouses, compared to 7 percent of the nonbattered women.[20] Eighty-five percent of the battered women reported that the sex was unpleasant for the following reasons: (1) it was initiated to prevent abuse, (2) took place immediately after battering to calm the batterer, (3) occurred after the abusive spouse abused a child for fear he would continue, and (4) refusing sex meant the battered woman would not be given money for groceries or bills.

Other researchers support the relationship between battering and conjugal rape. K. Yllo held that forced sex was a form of violent power and control rather than a means for sexual gratification.[21] David Finkelhor, co-author of a book on marital rape, noted of rape by husbands: "These are brutal acts that are most often committed out of anger or power, with the idea to humiliate, demean or degrade the wife."[22]

In using a conservative definition of marital rape that included forced intercourse with penetration, Russell found that marital rape occurred more than twice as often as stranger perpetrated rape. This suggested that battered women stood a risk of being sexually assaulted at a rate 3 to 5 times that of nonbattered women.[23]

Currently at least 11 states have made marital rape a crime, with a number of states headed in the same direction.

Sexual Jealousy Many battered women report that sexual problems such as frigidity, impotency, denial, and excessive demands lead to arguments and confrontations which erupt into physical violence.[24] In such cases, the abuser usually doubts his own virility and questions his wife's faithfulness, even at times questioning the paternity of his children. As a result, often the batterer forbids or severely curtails his wife's activities outside the home. Because of the brutality, many women feel alienated from their husbands and find sexual intimacy difficult—both of which only perpetuate the abuse.

The wife is also jealous of her husband at times, which may in turn trigger violent confrontations either borne out of denial or defense by the male.

Pregnancy and Battering When women have cited pregnancy as a factor in wife abuse, the most common explanation has been the added strain put on the relationship. This has proven to be especially true when it is an unplanned pregnancy. Jealousy and resentment toward the unborn child are often precipitating factors in the abuse. When the relationship is already strained by other sexual problems, unemployment, etc., a pregnancy can add to the strain and increase the likelihood of violence. Walker[25] and Gelles[26] reported a high degree of battering during first, second and third pregnancies. In Walker's study, 50 percent of the batterers were said to be initially pleased with the pregnancy but it did not prevent the abuse.

Wife battering has been in existence since ancient times, often thought of as an acceptable and even expected practice.

Sexual Intimacy Sex and intimacy appear to be related to wife battering in two ways. One is the relationship between battering and victim withdrawal from sexual intimacy as a consequence. According to Roy, this abuse and withdrawal often begin very early in the relationship.[27] The women she studied expressed feelings of worthlessness and alienation from their abusive husbands. This low self-esteem due to the battering made sexual intimacy difficult for the woman to achieve. Roy cited that accusations by the husband of infidelity and adultery by the wife contributed to the sexual problems and the battering.

A second correlation between sexual intimacy and battering exists in behavioral patterns of battered women and their inability to distinguish between sex and intimacy.[28] Following are reasons found why abused women have sexual relations with their abusive husbands:

• Seduction as an unrealistic sense of power.
• In order to keep the peace.
• Intense concentration on survival.

- Dependency upon an abusive though occasionally loving man.
- Joy from an intense intimate relationship.
- Knowledge of how to decrease the spouse's abusive behavior through a loving relationship.

Many such abused women may have been sexually abused during childhood. Walker advanced that "it is quite possible that early exposure to sexual abuse, with or without accompanying physical violence, creates a dependency upon the positive aspects of the intense intimacy experienced prior to the beginning of the battering behavior and continuing during the third phase of loving-kindness."[29]

Psychological abuse

Recent years have seen a greater emphasis placed on another form of woman battering that is just as detrimental to the woman's health and well being: psychological or emotional abuse.

In its broadest sense, psychological abuse can be defined as mistreatment in the form of threats, intimidation, isolation, degradation, mind games; and directing violence toward other family members or household objects (e.g., slamming doors). The first research project on psychological abuse in marriage in the United States was done by Patricia Hoffman, a psychologist at the St. Cloud State University Counseling Center in Minnesota. Hoffman defines this type of abuse as "behavior sufficiently threatening to a woman that she believes her capacity to work, to interact in the family or society, or to enjoy good physical or mental health, has been or might be endangered."[30]

Unfortunately there is no real way to measure the prevalence of psychological abuse of women, particularly when one takes into account the many women who remain silent, as well as those who may not even recognize that they are being psychologically violated. Notes Walker, as far back as the early 1970s when the number of refugees in England increased, "it became obvious that large numbers of women were seeking safety from psychological abuse."[31]

In a study of physical and psychological coerciveness, Walker found that both forms of abuse were present in assaultive couples and "cannot be separated, despite the difficulty in documentation."[32] Hoffman estimated, based on her study, that as many as 1 in 3 women may be involved in a psychologically abusive relationship.[33]

Marriage counselor Jeanne Weigum contends that psychological abuse of women is the underlying problem in the majority of dysfunctional relationships. "Women come in for counseling feeling unhappy," says Weigum. "But when they examine that unhappiness, it usually turns out that their husbands are practicing some form of psychological abuse."[34]

Explaining abusive men

Much research has gone into trying to understand the abusive man and why he strikes out at the one perhaps closest to him—his wife or significant other. Psychologists have characterized batterers in terms of adhering to a traditional male role or having a weak, immature personality.

Enactment of compulsive masculinity, often referred to as "machismo," is an effort to maintain complete dominance over his wife. On the other extreme, many batterers' personalities contain elements of helplessness and dependency. The violent husband has been characterized as a "little boy wanting to be grown up and superior, as he'd been taught he should be."[35]

Batterers have been described as "intractable" or "treatable," depending upon their perception of the violent behavior. "The intractable abuser finds no fault in his abusive action, whereas the treatable husband experiences guilt and remorse after the violence. In the latter instance, it is possible that with counseling the offender can learn nonviolent means of coping."[36]

Abusive Backgrounds Often both victims and abusers tend to come from violent backgrounds. Some studies have found that half the men who abuse women were themselves abused or witnessed family violence.[37] Batterers are more likely to come from abusive homes than battered women. Bonnie Carlson found that only one-third of the abused wives in her sample came from families where wife abuse had occurred.[38] J. Gayford's study found that 23 of 100 battered women had come from violent homes.[39]

Social Structure Theory Social structure theory holds that male violence is a reflection of particular structural and situational stimuli.[40] In order for violence to occur, two conditions must be met: (1) situational or structural stress must be present, and (2) the potential batterer must have been socialized to view violence as an appropriate response to certain situations, such as frustration.

Murray Straus identifies nine ways in which the "male-dominant structure of the society and of the family create and maintain a high level of marital violence"[41]:

- The defense of male authority.
- Compulsive masculinity.
- Economic constraints and discrimination.
- Difficulties in child care.
- The preeminence for women of the wife role.
- The single-parent household myth.
- The woman's negative self-image.
- The conception of women as children.
- The male orientation of the criminal justice system.

Lee Bowker advanced that "these values and norms bind women into a position in which they are easily victimized at the same time that they encourage men to flex their muscles."[42]

Why do women remain with an abusive mate?

The question of why physically or emotionally battered women tolerate this mistreatment has been probed perhaps more than any other question associated with wife abuse. On the surface it would seem to walk away from this anguish would be as simple as the front door. Some women do just that. And yet all too often, escaping an abusive spouse or boyfriend is far more difficult to do. There are a number of typical reasons ascribed for this, including:

- *Fear*—of the abuser, being humiliated, having others find out, being left alone.

- *Finances*—losing money, the house, standard of living.
- *Children*—losing financial support for them and a father.[43]
- *Social stigma*—shame, embarrassment, being labeled.
- *Guilt*—for bringing about the abuse or in believing that they are too needed by the abuser to leave.
- *Role expectations*—that abuse is a normal part of relationships; often based on learned experiences in childhood.

A cycle theory of violence has been developed by Lenore Walker as to why women remain in habitually abusive relationships.[44] The tension reduction theory advances that three specific phases exist in a recurring cycle of battering: (1) tension building, (2) the acute battering incident, and (3) loving contrition.

Women can be victimized by their mates in many ways, each of which can be devastating.

The tension stage consists of a series of minor or verbal attacks. The woman manages to cope with these episodes by minimizing their significance and/or severity and using anger reduction techniques. She seeks to appease the batterer by doing whatever is necessary to calm him down, in the process becoming even more submissive.

The second stage, the acute battering incident, is characterized by "the uncontrollable discharge of the tensions that have been built up during stage one." Typically the batterer unleashes both physical and verbal aggression upon the wife, which she is unable to prevent. It is in this phase of the cycle that most injuries, sometimes severe, take place.

The third stage is that of loving contrition or the "honeymoon period." The abuser becomes at once charming, loving, apologetic, kind, remorseful—in short, he takes a 180 degree turn and is willing to do anything to be forgiven. "Suddenly he's giving her gifts, good sex, pampering," says marriage and family counselor Laura Schlessinger. "She wants to believe he's really sorry and that he will change this time. In the glow of all this attention, she does believe it."[45] It is this contrition stage that provides the reinforcement for the woman remaining in the relationship. However, almost inevitably, stage one tension building resumes and a new cycle takes place.

Self-defense for the battered woman

For many battered women the only means of dealing with an abusive mate is to strike back violently. There are few statistics on male victims of spouse abuse, yet some researchers have found the incidence of female batterers to be significant. Robert Langley and Richard Levy estimated that 12 million men are physically abused by their wives in the United States during some point in their marriage.[46] Suzanne Steinmetz, author of an article titled "The Battered Husband Syndrome," estimated that 280,000 men in this country are battered each year.[47] Another study of spouse abuse findings approximated that 2 million husbands, compared to 1.8 million wives, had experienced at least one of the more serious forms of spouse abuse.[48]

This data notwithstanding, few believe that female batterers can measure up to male batterers in numbers or severity of violence. Rebecca Dobash and Russell Dobash found the ratio of male-to-female spouse abuse to be 66 to 1.[49]

Most experts agree that the battering of women has reached epidemic proportions.

Murders in Self-Defense In relatively rare instances, the battered woman is driven to the ultimate measure of self-defense—killing her abusive mate. Recent studies show that wives constitute more than half of the murdered spouses annually, with husbands being 6 to 7 times more likely to kill than be killed.[50] Female perpetrators of spouse homicide have been documented. In a study of homicides and attempted homicides by females in Hungary, it was found that 40 percent of the victims were husbands, common-law husbands, and lovers.[51] A similar finding was made by J. Totman in a study of 120 female murderers in the United States, where 40 percent of the women had killed husbands and lovers.[52] A study of females imprisoned for murder revealed that they were the sole perpetrators in 77 percent of the homicides, and in more than half of the homicides, the victim was an intimate or family member.[53] According to FBI figures, 4 percent of the male murder victims in the United States in 1992 were killed by a wife or girlfriend.[54]

Recent years have seen high profile cases of women killing their husbands or lovers with the motive often being self-defense after years of being the victim of spouse abuse. In a study of women charged with murder in Los Angeles County, Nancy Kaser-Boyd and Michael Maloney found that 42 percent of the women had killed a spouse or boyfriend.[55] Three-quarters of the women cited years of physical and psychological abuse at the hands of the victims. Another study of females imprisoned in a California penitentiary for murder found that 28 of the 30 women convicted of killing their spouses had been victims of wife battering.[56]

In *The Battered Woman Syndrome*, Walker gives a perspective on battered women turned murderers:

> Most women who killed their batterers have little memory of any cognitive processes other than an intense focus on their own survival. . . . Their description of the final incident indicates that they separate those angry feelings by the psychological process of a dissociative state. . . . This desperate attempt at remaining unaware of their own unacceptable feelings is a measure of just how dangerous they perceive their situation. They fear showing anger will cause their own death, and indeed it could as batterers cannot tolerate the woman's expression of anger.

The battered woman who kills her abuser is often so consumed with hopelessness, helplessness, despair, and low self-esteem that she is unable to think beyond the desperation of the moment until the deed is done and the ramifications already set in motion as a consequence. In the article "Women and Homicide," writer Elissa Benedek speaks of the point of no return typical of many battered homicidal women: "The battered wife has turned to social agencies, police, prosecutors, friends, ministers, and family, but they have not offered meaningful support or advice. . . . Abused women who have murdered their spouses reveal that they feel that homicide was the only alternative left to them."[58]

Sadly, battered women who kill their mates then become further victims as they often face murder charges, imprisonment, loss of their children, and lack of sympathy and understanding from the very social agencies that abandoned them in their hour of need.

Breaking the cycle of battering

Short of killing their abusers, breaking the cycle of abusive treatment at the hands of husbands and lovers is perhaps the most difficult aspect of the battered woman's syndrome. Psychologist Ann McClenahan explains: "The longer a woman stays and the harder she works to make the marriage work, the harder it is to leave."[59]

Battered women's shelters have been established throughout the country as a first step in escaping the abuse and abuser. These shelters offer refuge, counseling, and protection for battered women. More efforts are needed to get abused women to use such facilities for their safety and more shelters are sorely needed.

Criminal justice system agencies are better equipped in the nineties to deal with issues of family violence, and abusive men are more likely to serve time if charges are pressed. Nevertheless, law enforcement continues to fall short as an effective intervention to domestic violence, particularly wife abuse, which is often still looked upon as a private spousal matter. Most such cases fail to come to the attention of law enforcement, while laws are inconsistent from state to state. In fact, battered women must often take the initiative to escape the violence which, unfortunately, many victims are unable or unwilling to do.

Notes

1. Caroline Harlow, *Female Victims of Violent Crime* (Washington, D.C.: Office of Justice Programs, 1991), p. 1.

2. Terry Davidson, "Wifebeating: A Recurring Phenomenon Throughout History," as cited in Maria Roy, *The Abusive Partner: An Analysis of Domestic Battering* (New York: Van Nostrand Reinhold, 1982), p. 12.

3. Friedrich Engels, *The Origin of Family Private Property and the State* (Moscow: Progress Publishers, 1948), pp. 53–58

4. Ronald B. Flowers, *Women and Criminality: The Woman as Victim, Offender, and Practitioner* (Westport, Conn.: Greenwood Press, 1987), p. 15.

5. Flowers, *Women and Criminality*, p. 15; R. Calvert, "Criminal and Civil Liability in Husband-Wife Assaults," in Suzanne K. Steinmetz and Murray Straus, eds., *Violence in the Family* (New York: Dodd, Mead, 1975), p. 89.

6. Mildred D. Pagelow, *Woman Battering: Victims and Their Experiences* (Beverly Hills: Sage Publications, 1981), p. 33.

7. Ronald B. Flowers, *Demographics and Criminality: The Characteristics of Crime in America* (Westport, Conn.: Greenwood Press, 1989), pp. 151–160.

8. Suzanne K. Steinmetz, *The Cycle of Violence: Assertive, Aggressive, and Abusive Family Interaction* (New York: Praeger Publishers, 1977).

9. Lenore E. Walker, "Treatment Alternatives for Battered Women," in Jane R. Chapman and Margaret Gates, eds., *The Victimization of Women* (Beverly Hills: Sage Publications, 1978), p. 144.

10. Diana E. Russell, *Rape in Marriage* (New York: Macmillan, 1982).

11. Cited in Judith Levine, "Crimes Against Women Are Growing and So Are Our Fears," *Glamour* (February, 1986), p. 210.

12. Frances Patai, "Pornography and Woman Battering: Dynamic Similarities," in Maria Roy, ed., *The Abusive Partner*, p. 92.

13. *Ibid.*

14. U.S. Federal Bureau of Investigation, *Crime in the United States: Uniform Crime Reports 1992* (Washington, D.C.: Government Printing Office, 1993), p. 17.

15. Flowers, *Women and Criminality*, pp. 15–16.

16. Terry Davidson, *Conjugal Crime: Understanding and Changing the Wife-Beating Pattern* (New York: Hawthorne, 1979).

17. Maria Roy, "Four Thousand Partners in Violence: A Trend Analysis," in Maria Roy, ed., *The Abusive Partner*, pp. 34–35.

18. Harlow, *Female Victims*, p. 7.

19. "Marital Rape: Drive for Tougher Laws Is Pressed," *New York Times* (May 13, 1987), p. A16.

20. Lenore E. Walker, *The Battered Woman Syndrome* (New York: Springer, 1984), pp. 48–49.

21. K. Yllo, *Types of Marital Rape: Three Case Studies*, presented at the National Conference for Family Violence Researchers, University of New Hampshire, Durham, July 1981.

22. Cited in "Marital Rape," p. A16.

23. Russell, *Rape in Marriage.*

24. Roy, "Four Thousand Partners," pp. 31-32.

25. Walker, *The Battered Woman Syndrome*, p. 51.

26. Richard J. Gelles, "Violence and Pregnancy: A Note on the Extent of the Problem and Needed Services," *Family Coordinator* 24 (1975): 81–86.

27. Roy, "Four Thousand Partners," p. 32.

28. Flowers, *Women and Criminality*, pp. 19–20.

29. Walker, *The Battered Woman Syndrome*, p. 55.

30. Quoted in Cheryll Ostrom, "The Battle Scars of Emotional Abuse," *Sacramento Bee* (October 29, 1986), p. B1.

31. Walker, *The Battered Woman Syndrome.*

32. *Ibid.*

33. Cited in Ostrom, "The Battle Scars," p. B1.

34. *Ibid.*

35. Flowers, *Women and Criminality*, p. 20; Kathleen H. Hofeller, *Social, Psychological, and Situational Factors in Wife Abuse* (Palo Alto, Calif.: R & E Research Associates, 1982), p. 39.

36. Flowers, *Women and Criminality*, p. 20; Davidson, *Conjugal Crime*, p. 23.

37. Hofeller, *Social, Psychological, and Situational Factors*, p. 43.

38. Bonnie E. Carlson, "Battered Women and Their Assailants," *Social Work* 22, 6 (1977): 456.

39. J. Gayford, "Wife Battering: A Preliminary Survey of 100 Cases," *British Medical Journal* 1 (1975): 194–197.

40. Richard J. Gelles, *The Violent Home: A Study of the Physical Aggression Between Husbands and Wives* (Beverly Hills: Sage Publications, 1972).

41. Murray A. Straus, "Sexual Inequality, Cultural Norms, and Wife-Beating," *Victimology* 1 (1976): 62–66.

42. Lee H. Bowker, *Women, Crime, and the Criminal Justice System* (Lexington, Mass.: Lexington Books, 1978), p. 128.

43. Studies show that only around 1 in 3 fathers totally complies with court ordered child support during the first year after divorce. By the 10th year of divorce, only 13 percent of the fathers pay full child support, while nearly 8 out of 10 fathers pay no child support at all after 10 years.

44. Walker, *The Battered Woman Syndrome*.

45. Cited in Nancy Baker, "Why Women Stay with Men Who Beat Them," *Glamour* (August 1983), p. 366.

46. Robert Langley and Richard C. Levy, *Wife Beating: The Silent Crisis* (New York: E. P. Dutton, 1977).

47. Suzanne K. Steinmetz, "The Battered Husband Syndrome," *Victimology* 2 (1978): 507.

48. Richard J. Gelles, "The Myth of Battered Husbands," *Ms.* (October 1979): 65–72.

49. Rebecca Dobash and Russell Dobash, *Violence Against Wives* (New York: Free Press, 1979).

50. K. Yllo and Murray A. Straus, "Interpersonal Violence Among Married and Cohabitating Couples," paper presented at the annual meeting of the National Council on Family Relations, Philadelphia, 1978.

51. G. Rasko, "The Victim of the Female Killer," *Victimology* 1 (1976): 396–402.

52. J. Totman, *The Murderess: A Psychological Study of the Process* (Ann Arbor: University Microfilms, 1971).

53. D. Ward, M. Jackson, and R. Ward, "Crimes of Violence by Women," in D. Mulvihill, M. M. Tamin, and L. A. Curtis, eds., *Crimes of Violence* (Washington, D. C.: Government Printing Office, 1969).

54. *Uniform Crime Reports*, p. 17.

55. Cited in Sandy Nelson, "Women Who Kill," *Sacramento Bee* (December 30, 1986), p. B9.

56. Cited in Nick Jordan, "Till Murder Us Do Part," *Psychology Today* (July 1985), p. 7.

57. Walker, *The Battered Woman Syndrome*, p. 40.

58. Cited in Glen Collins, "A Study Assesses Traits of Women Who Kill," *New York Times* (July 7, 1986), p. C18.

59. Quoted in Ostrom, "The Battle Scars of Emotional Abuse," p. B1.

2

Domestic Violence Is a Serious Problem for Women

Erica Goode et al.

Erica Goode is a staff writer for U.S. News & World Report, *a weekly newsmagazine.*

Every year in the United States, thousands of men assault their wives and girlfriends, raising both physical and emotional bruises from which some women never recover. Some women die from the attacks. Others escape their abuser only to be hunted down and killed.

This is how it happens: Inside a quiet room, behind a closed door, a man calls a woman a "slut" and a "whore." He tells her that she is too fat or too sexy or too frumpy, that she is "a poor excuse for a mother," a worthless piece of dirt that only he could love. In public, when she smiles at the grocery clerk, he flies into a jealous rage. When she comes home minutes late, he grills her about where she's been. One day, he slaps her face. The next time, he slams her head against the wall, or chokes her, or burns her with cigarettes, or drags her across the rug by her hair, his children pleading, "Daddy, please don't hurt her." Then, when it's over, he gets down on his knees. "I'm so sorry, baby," he says. "You're the only one I can talk to. I'll kill myself if you leave." Quivering with shame and fear, she relents. And one day, perhaps after she has finally tried to break off the relationship, she ends up dead. It may have happened to Nicole Simpson. [Nicole Simpson was murdered on June 12, 1994. Her ex-husband, O.J. Simpson, was arrested and tried for the murder.] It happens to 1,400 to 2,500 women in America each year.

For decades, domestic-violence workers have pleaded with the public to take family violence seriously. They have pointed to inadequacies in state and federal laws, to systematic neglect by police, prosecutors and judges, to meager funding for overburdened hot lines and shelters, to the absence of protection for women in mortal danger. They have recited the statistics of abuse: 100,000 hospitalization days each year; 30,000 emergency room visits; an estimated 2 million incidents of battering, male and

Erica Goode, "Till Death Do Them Part?" *U.S. News & World Report*, July 4, 1994; ©1994, U.S. News & World Report. Reprinted with permission.

female. They have explained the complex web of emotional manipulation, physical intimidation and financial dependence that imprisons victims, hoping that the question "Why does she stay so long?" will eventually be replaced by more useful queries.

Yet it may be a single gruesome murder, with the hurricane of publicity surrounding it, that finally makes Americans pay attention. As evidence against O.J. Simpson was presented to a Los Angeles grand jury, later called off the case by a judge, calls flooded domestic-violence hot lines and resource centers across the country. Stories of battered women filled newspaper columns and flickered across television screens, transcripts of Nicole Simpson's desperate calls to 911 during her ex-husband's attacks providing a chilling obbligato. "The Simpson case is the equivalent of Anita Hill's sexual harassment charges," says Temple University School of Law Professor Marina Angel. "Because of this case, people will become more aware of what abused women go through."

Changing the system

This heightened awareness is translating into legislative fervor and spurring increased demands for effective enforcement of current laws. New York State lawmakers agreed to endorse a bill requiring mandatory arrest for anyone suspected of severe battering or violating a protective order—a law already on the books in 25 other states. In Chicago, six women recently filed suit in U.S. District Court, charging that police failed to protect them against their abusers and asking $15 million in damages. Susan Murphy Milano, whose Chicago-based group, Project Protect, organized the suit, plans to file similar actions in other states. And federal officials, led by Attorney General Janet Reno, urged support for the federal crime bill, which would earmark several hundred million dollars in new domestic-violence funding for states and localities, including money for programs encouraging arrests of abusers, better treatment programs, "family violence courts" and restoration of a national, toll-free hot line, discontinued in 1992.

Yet the safety of millions of victims, domestic-violence experts say, depends ultimately on a cultural shift much larger than any law can guarantee. Indeed, the blood was barely dry on the pavement outside Nicole Simpson's home when a woman made a frantic call to a domestic-violence hot line in central Pennsylvania: Her husband, she said, was threatening to "O.J. her."

For decades, domestic-violence workers have pleaded with the public to take family violence seriously.

In the face of such incidents, the truth is that the burden of women's safety falls largely on the shoulders of women themselves. They can educate themselves about resources in their communities, find out what they can expect from the legal system and what they can't, learn to recognize the warning signs that a person is capable of physical aggression. If forced to go into hiding from abusive partners, they can maximize the chances that they will remain undetected. And most of all, they can begin to rebuild their shattered self-esteem. "It's never too late to get out," says Margarete Hintz, a Pennsylvania woman who says she left her husband after 38 years of abuse. "I had strength I never thought I had."

"He said, 'I am the boss and I will always be the boss. I own you.'"

Patrina Sims, abuse victim

No woman knowingly falls in love with a man who will abuse her: She falls in love with a man who is often charming and charismatic and who says the things that Hollywood and years of socialization have taught her are the hallmarks of true love. "I want you all to myself," he tells her. "You are my queen. I've never met anyone who understands me like you do." Not infrequently, the couple marries or moves in together after a short and intense courtship. She only realizes later that his adoration comes wrapped in jealousy and controlling behavior. "He was jealous of anybody I spent time with or knew," says Patricia Howard, one of the six women in the Chicago lawsuit, of an ex-boyfriend who she says raped and beat her. "I couldn't say hello to anyone—male or female—without him jumping all over my case." Howard's experience is typical: "An abuser will always say that jealousy is a sign of love," advises a 17-point brochure, "Signs to Look for in a Battering Personality," available from the San Diego Police Department's domestic-violence unit. The longer a woman knows a man before moving in with him, domestic-violence experts add, the better her chances of recognizing the potential for violence before it occurs.

> *The safety of millions of victims . . . depends ultimately on a cultural shift much larger than any law can guarantee.*

Domestic abuse is a high-stakes game of control, and batterers are expert players. Both the batterer and his victim may have grown up in homes in which they were physically abused or witnessed abuse. Each has absorbed distorted lessons: The man, who may have seen his father beat his mother, learns that aggression is a sign of manliness. For her part, the woman may believe the abuse is her fault, having seen her mother take on the blame, and perhaps her grandmother before that. One woman, who went to her grandmother covered with bruises from her husband's beatings, was told: "You have to stop provoking him. You have two children, and the bottom line is, you have nowhere to go. If he tells you to shut up, shut up."

"Do not keep quiet about this! It's everybody's responsibility in your community."

Donna Ferrato, photographer and founder
of the Domestic Abuse Awareness Project

A good marriage is a refuge, its privacy a buffer against the world. For the abused woman, the marital bond becomes an isolating nightmare. Abusers exploit this, actively tearing apart the woman's support network, pushing friends and family away. If she has male friends, he may harass them or punish her for being a "flirtatious bitch." If she has women friends, he may say they are lesbians or treat them so rudely they become reluctant to visit. And because abused women frequently feel embarrassed and ashamed, they are apt to let friendships go rather than share their dark secret.

Yet silence, domestic-violence experts say, is what keeps batterers in business. It can ultimately prove deadly. The first time a woman is hit, she should immediately tell someone, says Catrina Steinocher, director of programming at the Corpus Christi Women's Shelter in Texas, cautioning that victims should also expect that some friends and family members will not be supportive. If a woman encountering her partner's violence for the first time is not prepared to leave, she should at the very least find a family violence shelter in her area where she can obtain counseling and education.

No woman knowingly falls in love with a man who will abuse her.

If the experience of many abuse victims is any indication, even this first step may take some diligent work. Police stations can usually provide phone numbers and locations of local shelters. Directory assistance may also have listings, although in many cities the woman must know the name of the shelter to obtain the number. Massachusetts recently passed a law requiring 411 operators to provide the number of a shelter in the caller's area, but many regions lag far behind in this service. Some organizations offer toll-free hot lines that operate during limited hours.

"If violence occurs once . . . it will happen again."

San Diego Police Department safety plan

Intelligent, well-meaning people often ask why women stay in abusive relationships. Yet the real question is how so many women muster the courage to leave. Batterers tend to escalate their violence in proportion to the victim's attempts to become independent—walking out can mean risking serious injury or even death. Unless a woman has made a careful plan, she may not have either the means to support herself or a safe place to stay. Her self-esteem systematically chipped away, her children in need of a father, for a while it may seem less difficult to suffer another black eye or bruised rib. Most imprisoning, however, is the knowledge that if she leaves, she loses. "I stayed because when I left, I left everything I owned or loved," says Vickii Coffey, now executive director of the Chicago Abused Women Coalition, who was abused by her ex-husband. "I left a house that was paid for, a car that was paid for. I left with two suitcases, two children and $1,500 to start over again."

The best course, domestic-violence experts say, is for a woman to leave immediately the first time her partner hits her. But if she chooses to stay, there are steps she can take to increase her safety. If an argument begins, she can try to move it away from the kitchen or bathroom—where knives and other potential weapons are readily at hand—and into a room with an outside door, offering the possibility of escape. She can pick a code word—something unusual, like "cantaloupe"—and rehearse it with her children, friends, neighbors and family. When the code word is used, it means "Call the police." She can also pack a bag, keeping it in a hidden but accessible place, in case she needs to leave quickly, and install more than one telephone or buy a cordless phone, so that if one unit is disabled, she can use another to call the police.

Every woman's situation is unique, every batterer has different triggers and the victim herself is the best judge of what will put her in danger. Shelter workers will help her devise a safety plan tailored to her situation. If she is preparing to leave, they may advise her, among other things, to open her own savings account, to find people who will let her stay with them or lend her money, to memorize the number of a shelter and to plan ahead by leaving an extra set of keys, extra clothes and important documents—birth certificates, passports, driver's license, restraining orders—with someone she trusts.

> *"I can't sleep. I might fall asleep, but in five minutes I'll awaken from a dream of running from this man or this man coming in on me."*
>
> Cassandra Finley, in hiding from the
> ex-boyfriend she says stalked and shot her

Batterers have many responses to the departure of their victim. Some let her go. Others beg her to come back, call her on the telephone, perhaps harass her for a while, but eventually leave her alone, allowing her to start a new life. Yet, there are some men who cannot ever let go and will stalk a victim using any means possible to track her down. In response, the woman becomes a fugitive, trying to outguess the batterer's every move.

A woman running from a batterer must turn her life inside out. She must change her daily routines; take a different route to the grocery store and the preschool; park in a different parking space; put safety guards on doors and windows, even on upper floors; distribute a recent photo of her batterer to coworkers and neighbors, and instruct them to call the police if they spot an unusual car or hear suspicious noises. She must beware of solicitors, refuse telephone surveys and notify telephone and electric companies of her danger so that they do not give her away. She must take a hundred other steps to protect herself as well, working out her plans in advance with a shelter or domestic-violence counselor.

Batterers tend to escalate their violence in proportion to the victim's attempts to become independent.

It is no panacea for women to have batterers arrested or seek civil protective orders against them. But either action may help, forcing the batterer instead of the victim to leave and giving authorities more leverage in prosecuting the abuser. Police officers and judges gradually are becoming trained in handling domestic-violence cases, but many women still face resistance from unsympathetic officials, and enforcement of protective orders remains problematic. Some courts now order additional protection, making batterers wear electronic bracelets, an alarm sounding in the victim's home if he gets too close, or providing "panic alarms," which allow victims to summon help silently.

In the end, though, it is up to the woman to take the precautions she needs to survive—the irony, of course, being that she has done nothing wrong. "The danger," says Elizabeth Dillon, domestic-violence liaison for the Cambridge, Massachusetts, Police Department, "is that at some point, a victim may say, 'I can't do this anymore.'" One day, exhausted and stressed, she may lapse into old habits, taking a familiar road to work, going to the grocery store on her accustomed day. And that will be the day that he is there, waiting.

3

Domestic Violence Is a Serious Problem for Professional Women

Hillary Johnson

Hillary Johnson is a contributing writer for Working Woman *magazine, a monthly journal for professional women.*

The common belief that domestic violence occurs primarily in lower-income families is inaccurate. Professional women with good jobs and financial security also find themselves in abusive relationships with men. In many cases, these women find dealing with the problem even more difficult than poor women do because the violence is more unexpected and they are often less willing to utilize the social services that could help them escape from their abuser.

For most people, the phrase "domestic violence" summons a stereotypical scene: police pounding on the door of a ramshackle house; a man loudly, perhaps drunkenly, declaring his innocence; a woman crying. But for a vast number of middle- or upper-class women, many of them professionals, domestic violence is a secret, usually silent affair. They are prisoners of their world, but for many reasons they feel compelled to don a mask of normalcy. In spite of their bruises and scars, they may not even admit that they are victims. And until they fully acknowledge what is happening to them—a process that can take years—the very last thing they want to do is make their situation public.

Definitive statistics on these white-collar victims are hard to come by, especially because shame or fear of reprisal makes them reluctant to report the crime. The Justice Department's 1994 National Crime Victimization Survey (NCVS) found that only about half the women who suffered domestic abuse between 1987 and 1991 reported it to the police. As incredible as it may seem, *Family Violence: Crime and Justice*, a 1989 book that reviewed the research on the subject, projected that one-fifth to one-

Hillary Johnson, "The Truth About White-Collar Domestic Violence." This article first appeared in *Working Woman* in March 1995; ©1995 by *Working Woman* magazine. It is reprinted by permission of *Working Woman* magazine.

third of all women could be assaulted by an intimate at some point. And the perception that most victims are poor and uneducated is clearly distorted. The NCVS found less than a 10% difference in the rate of family violence between those with household incomes of less than $10,000 and those earning more than $50,000. "Women of means are just as trapped as women on welfare," says Carol Arthur, the director of the Domestic Abuse Project in Minneapolis, a nonprofit program that aids victims. "The stories and issues are all the same. There are just different barriers to leaving the relationship."

For a vast number of middle- or upper-class women, many of them professionals, domestic violence is a secret, usually silent affair.

Perhaps the greatest myth about white-collar domestic violence is that its victims should be able to arrange smooth, bloodless departures because, unlike poor women, they are blessed with financial and social resources. "The irony is how hard it can be even for women who earn more than the men they're involved with to leave," says Sharon Rice Vaughn, who cofounded one of the first battered-women's shelters in the country in 1972 in St. Paul. "It is particularly hard for professional, highly paid women to believe that battering is happening to *them*." One TV reporter was blind to the warning signs in her own relationship even though she had covered a number of domestic-violence cases. "I was in denial that I could be an abused woman because I'm smart, I'm professional, I know a lot of cops," she says. "And there was this constant self-questioning—is it really as bad as I think it is?" Experts say the confusion is compounded by a *Gaslight* [a movie by Alfred Hitchcock in which a husband schemes to convince his wife that she is going insane] effect created by the sporadic, random nature of the abuse; the victim wonders whether she really is being brutalized or whether the attacks are somehow her fault. The effect is even more potent when there's a strong desire to keep the relationship intact. "It's about *wanting* it to be a one-time thing," notes a domestic-abuse counselor.

In addition, professional women are trapped by a fear of exposure. "That's the abuser's secret emotional blackmail," says Rice Vaughn. "If you have a reputation, your reputation will be ruined." In fact, women who earn more or are more successful than their partners can be more vulnerable targets than women of like status to their husbands', according to Evan Stark, co-director of the Domestic Violence Training Project in New Haven, 40% of whose clients are middle- and upper-class victims of domestic abuse. "Those men are compensating by resorting to socially condoned male dominance," explains Rice Vaughn. "It becomes their form of revenge. It's as though she is being blamed for his failures—if she weren't so successful, he wouldn't be seen as less successful."

Lorraine Holmes, an attorney in Homestead, Florida, represents mainly women who have been battered or otherwise abused by their husbands. Holmes herself lived with an abusive man in South Florida for four years beginning in 1984 while attempting to build her law career. She was the wage earner, he the househusband who assured her he would soon "make it big" in the music business. "I always counsel women to make an escape plan," says Holmes. "If it means saving only $3 to $4 a week from the household money, *do* it." Her own plan involved confronting her former husband—although she knew the result would be injury to herself—during an 18-month trial "pro-arrest period" in greater Miami. She arranged a two-week absence from work, then informed her husband of her intent to divorce him. "He dragged me across the floor, threw me into a wall and threatened to kill me. I had handprint bruises on my arms and an abrasion on my face, but I don't remember whether it was from him hitting me or slamming me into the wall."

Afterward, Holmes slipped away to a neighbor's and called the police. Her husband spent three nights in jail, giving Holmes time to get a protection order and, she adds, a gun. Her husband violated the order by contacting her by telephone. Now, despite her flourishing practice, even the Florida Bar has access only to a post-office-box number. And although it has been over two years since she last heard from her ex-husband, she continues to live in fear. "I still believe he's capable of homicide," she says.

How did Holmes get involved with a violent man, and why did it take her four years to leave? Certainly, little about her suggests someone easily intimidated or willing to suffer abuse. During the 1970s, Holmes, who graduated in the top 7% of her law class, spent most of her time fighting for feminist causes. And her husband-to-be, like many abusers, showed no predilection toward violence throughout a five-month courtship; indeed, Holmes found him particularly seductive and charming. "He was the only man I had ever gone out with who was as smart as I was," Holmes says. "His sweet-talking got me hooked on the relationship. He had already started the crazy-making—convincing me I had no memory, that my recollections of conversations were wrong—but it was done very subtly. Despite one prior incident of abuse, I married him in May 1985."

Women who earn more or are more successful than their partners can be more vulnerable targets than women of like status to their husbands'.

Aside from the subtle manipulation, there were no warning signs that he was capable of severe physical violence. The first blow enraged Holmes: "I told him to get out of my life." Her reaction was typical of many women, says Evan Stark, "who have grown up with a certain level of entitlement—they're incensed. And at first they think they can control or change it. But with these manipulative men, you can be in a relationship for a *long* time before you get it together to leave." Stark points out that in many white-collar households, the violence is not just sporadic but rare; rather, the abuser depends on "coercive strategies—the use of intimidation and threats—to gain and keep control." Holmes allowed her husband to return when he convinced her that the violence had been a fluke. "When people like me, who are out to change the world, get into a relationship with someone who is so clearly disturbed, the crusading part of our personality comes out—we're going to fix that, too," she says.

Nevertheless, her husband steadily escalated the psychological harassment and abuse. "Batterers use the same techniques as terrorists," Holmes says. "Isolation, threats and random violence. I never knew whether I was coming home to a cooked meal and a bubble bath or to accusations and intimidating behavior, which may or may not have resulted in physical violence, like the meal being thrown in my face or him jabbing at my gut with a two-by-four."

In many white-collar households, . . . the abuser depends on "coercive strategies—the use of intimidation and threats—to gain and keep control."

Holmes wanted out by the end of the second year of marriage, but like many in her situation, she was demoralized and discouraged, as well she might have been: Statistics indicate that women who leave their abusive partners are at a 75% greater risk of being killed by their abusers than those who stay. "I've followed the news and seen a lot of domestic-homicide reports in Miami," says Holmes. "No one cared before Nicole Brown Simpson was killed—they were back-paged. I would just get up the courage to leave, and then I would read about another murder." Holmes's salvation came when she began meeting other victims of domestic assault at a counseling service offered by Dade County. "Most of these women had gotten free, and they were able to help me objectively assess the risk of mortality."

Although Holmes and some other women interviewed sought help through public agencies, many professional women suffer years of torment because they are isolated in their experience. Unlike poor women, who may have used other public services, professional, middle-class women can be loath to seek help from women's shelters. If they look for help, it is typically in the private offices of marriage counselors. But "marriage counseling assumes you're on a level playing field with your abuser," says Susan Neis, director of Cornerstone, an organization providing services to domestic-abuse victims in four affluent suburbs of Minneapolis. "You aren't."

Professional women usually have a great deal to lose by severing ties with their abusers, often including an expensive home in an exclusive neighborhood, their social standing in the community, their financial security and a superior education for their children. Because so much is riding on the perpetuation of their marriage, they may lack supporters— even among their own families. "Look at Nicole Brown Simpson," says Carol Arthur. "Her family was in business with O.J.! I have heard women weigh their safety with what they would give up. If the violence happens only three or four times a year, they barter."

There is also the problem of a legal system that one victim characterizes as an "abuser's haven." Women trying to divorce wealthy, established husbands typically find themselves ensnarled in court battles for years. Finally, the fact remains that when a man is intent upon killing his wife, there is no sure way to prevent it. One distinguished judge whose husband was arrested for assaulting her says, "I have not even tried to get a divorce, because I believe it would be fatal." She stipulated that she could not, under any circumstances, be identified. "Absence of malice," she says, in a reference to the libel defense, "won't help me when I'm dead."

Killing their careers

Aside from the physical and emotional toll, domestic violence can exert a crushing weight on a career. Holmes was just starting out in an elite Miami firm when her husband began his terrorist tactics. "He would physically restrain me from going to work," Holmes says. Once, stark naked, he pursued her out the front door and into the yard in order to pull her back inside. "Eventually," Holmes recalls, "I was barely out of the house before I would begin to be afraid of what would face me when I got home. It blew my concentration at work. In the corporate world, and certainly in the legal world, you're expected to perform at 120% no matter what. Toward the end, people were rewriting my briefs. I was told that I couldn't put together a cogent sentence."

Holmes discovered as well that a frank admission of an abusive relationship can deter prospective employers from hiring women. When she explained the gaps in her job history to employers, "they immediately assumed that if I was so weak as to allow myself to be abused, I would be a weak litigator," she says. It was one reason Holmes launched a solo practice.

Jeanne Raffesberger, a Wisconsinite, was an ambitious technical analyst in the insurance industry. Throughout a 15-year marriage, her husband repeatedly threatened her life with knives and, twice, with a .357 Magnum revolver. But, as with many working women married to abusers, it was the day-to-day psychological harassment that damaged her most. "He would call me stupid, tell me I was a miserable failure," she says. Some days her husband would prevent her from going to work by taking her car keys from her. Whenever she began to make progress in her career, he would demand that she quit her job, stay home and clean house—eight hours a day. At 2 PM she would fill the sinks and tubs with hot water and Pine Sol. When her husband arrived home later to the wafting aroma of pine, he was reassured that she had fulfilled her wifely duty to him. Nevertheless, within days he would order her to "get off her ass" and find work. "It was a gradual, incremental slide into total chaos," she remembers. She abandoned her career.

Many professional women suffer years of torment because they are isolated in their experience.

In a 1987 survey from the New York Victim Service Agency, three-quarters of 50 employed battered women reported being harassed by their abusers at work. And half of them reported missing three or more days a month because of their abuse. Another survey, conducted in Duluth, Minnesota, found that of 71 abused working women, nearly a quarter reported losing a job at least partly because of their abusive partners; in addition, one-third of 42 battered Duluth women reported that their partners had prohibited them from working altogether. Finally, because of the numerous daytime court appearances that may be required, particularly when child custody is at issue, victims of domestic violence are at risk of being penalized or fired for absenteeism, lateness or decreased productivity.

The powerful abuser

For professional women married to abusers who are also power brokers out to preserve their reputations, the road to freedom can be virtually endless—and carpeted with broken glass. Money offers these men a way to perpetuate the psychic pain through the courts; the more money, the more tools the abuser holds and the longer the battle rages.

Jenny Barry's marriage to Tom Barry followed a brief, intense courtship that left Jenny's friends envious of her seemingly remarkable fortune: Barry was a well-known retailer in a large southern city whose chain of clothing stores had made him a millionaire (the couple's names and identifying details have been changed). Jenny was a successful sculptor who had already had three one-woman shows in prominent local galleries. Not long after the wedding, Barry threw her against a wall when she asked him to hang up her coat.

Professional women usually have a great deal to lose by severing ties with their abusers.

"I moved out and told him I wouldn't come back until he got help," Jenny recalls. After two weeks, Barry's assurances that he would never again harm her lured her back. The next time, he tried to choke her. She spent eight days with a friend in Seattle. "He was like a time bomb—I never knew when he was going to blow—but afterward there was always great remorse." She didn't think of herself as a battered woman. After all, she was living in a million-dollar house with a very rich husband. And Barry's assaults were infrequent enough to keep her off guard. "I wasn't brutally beaten every week," Jenny recalls. "I was living with a bully." The chronic fear, she says, killed her creativity, and her career as an artist "came to a dead stop."

Eight years into the marriage, when she learned that Barry was still in contact with a former lover and had lied to her about it, Jenny sought a divorce. She didn't mention the physical abuse in her petition; she had simply come to accept that as a fact of the marriage. As the process began, Barry was allowed visitation with their 5-year-old daughter every other weekend. After one visit, the little girl revealed that Barry had touched her in what Jenny thought was a sexual way. Jenny's attorney suggested a physical exam; a pediatrician found that the child's injuries "could be consistent with an occurrence of sexual abuse." Barry denied the charges. The court found that "inappropriate sexual contact" had occurred, but awarded Barry continued shared custody since it did not appear to the court to be "part of a pattern of behavior" and there was "no future threat of abuse." In addition, the judge sealed the divorce records.

Jenny had borrowed $30,000 from her mother for legal fees and living expenses. Eventually her attorneys' fees topped $150,000, and she had to start representing herself. During the proceedings, she was told that she could remain in the house, but, she recalls, "Tom drained the equity by taking out loans against it for his businesses. The house went into foreclosure, and my daughter and I were given 48 hours to leave." The house was sold to one of Barry's business associates. In the end, Barry, who had declared liabilities exactly equal to his almost $4 million in assets, was awarded sole rights to all the businesses, plus all interest in pending projects and deals. Jenny was awarded a 1983 Volkswagen, their furniture and alimony of $2,500 a month for 10 years. Recently, she declared bankruptcy. Her daughter, now 11, continues to visit her father every other weekend.

Aside from the physical and emotional toll, domestic violence can exert a crushing weight on a career.

"First I was abused by Tom," Jenny says. "Then my daughter was abused by Tom. And then we were abused by the system."

Florida attorney Holmes calls these protracted legal frays "wars of attrition." "When the cash runs out, the attorneys withdraw," she says, leaving the woman the loser because she is usually unable to stand toe-to-toe with her abuser financially. "These guys are very slick at hiding assets. They've often done it throughout the marriage." Like Jenny Barry, some women resort to representing themselves, but, Holmes continues, "a *pro se* litigant stands virtually no chance of winning. I have never withdrawn from a domestic case when the money runs out, by the way, but I hand out a sheet to my clients telling them to expect that he will spend every penny on attorneys rather than give it to them or the children."

Some observers consider the plight of women who are victimized by such men qualitatively worse than that of women whose husbands, however brutal, lack the financial toolbox to manipulate the judicial system. "Society goes after the little guy," notes one victim, "but the big guys are clever, and they won't give up until they destroy you."

Leaving for the children

Most abused women experience a moment when they resolve to get out of the relationship at any cost. For Ann, an oncology nurse in the Northeast (her name, profession and location have been changed for her protection), that point came when her then-3-year-old son witnessed her husband hitting her in the throat and throwing her across a room. When her husband left the house afterward, she called a service for battered women at her mother's urging. "The feedback I got was, 'This will not get better.' I thought, 'I cannot have my son grow up thinking this is OK.' A moving van arrived six days later, and I was gone."

Ann and her son moved several states away, to her hometown. That was in 1991. Her husband, a computer expert, dragged the divorce proceedings on for two and a half years, unsuccessfully seeking sole custody of the child. A few months before a judge was to rule on alimony and child-support payments, he changed his $50,000-plus job to a half-time, half-salary, no-benefits position, a not-uncommon tactic that reduced Ann's anticipated support payments by about half.

For Ann, however, money was not the central issue. "The fear that he would manipulate the legal system in such a way that I would lose my child was almost incapacitating at times," she says. Ultimately, a judge ruled that the two would share legal custody. Then, 18 months ago, Ann's former husband moved within two miles of her house, ratcheting up her fear level by several notches. Unfortunately, there exists no safe neutral place where Ann can deliver her son to him under protection. She keeps her doors locked and her curtains drawn, and she uses caller ID. "When the doorbell rings, I have a physical response," she says. "When a car drives by, I look." Acknowledging that she is in danger every time she must take her son to her ex-husband, she says, "Prove that to the judge! No one believes you, because these guys have beautiful masks. There's nothing I would like more than to have legal justice in this situation, but this guy's too smart." After a moment, she adds, "It's the slow murder of the soul that goes on—and what judge is going to hear that? I sense that I could be in legal battles over my son until he's 18. He's 7 now."

Fortunately for Ann, she works in a hospital with sympathetic supervisors. Soon after her husband moved nearby, she began to get a lot of hang-up calls at home; so did the hospital ward to which she was assigned. Apparently, her ex-husband was attempting to decipher her work schedule. She no longer answers the telephone at work, and hospital officials have promised to protect her. "I work with some very compassionate people who understand about abuse, or are willing to learn, and they've been incredibly sensitive," she says. During Ann's first year on the job, the head nurse granted her time off to attend legal proceedings. She credits the people she works with for making her job her safe haven.

Although domestic violence discriminates along gender lines rather than class lines, professional women have one advantage over poor women: their job skills and education.

Most experts consider the issue of child custody and visitation one of the biggest problems, if not the biggest one, faced by women in domestic-violence cases. Only 40 states have statutes stipulating that domestic-violence charges may be presented in custody cases. In Evan Stark's opinion, shared custody is "completely inappropriate in domestic-abuse cases." He calls it "tangential spouse abuse," because the man typically uses the child to continue to exercise control over the woman with threats and psychological torture, and, in some cases, it gives him opportunities to physically abuse her.

The price of freedom

Like Ann, Jeanne Raffesberger was able to summon the courage to file for divorce only when, while beating her, her husband began beating their two young sons as well. Although there had been violence before, she, like numerous other women in her situation, did not identify herself as a battered woman until then. Afterward, her husband packed his workout bag and left for the gym. Raffesberger took her children and headed for a women's shelter. "I would live in a box under a bridge, I would panhandle, I would eat dog food—but I wouldn't live there anymore," she says.

The state prosecuted her husband only for child abuse. Meanwhile, Raffesberger hid from him, taking an apartment, buying her own car and getting an unlisted phone number. Released after serving 30 days in a work program, her husband was allowed supervised visits with his children and, eventually, unsupervised visits. "There was no way to facilitate a safe exchange," Raffesberger says, "and he found out where I lived."

Like many women who know their abusers well, she sensed one day that her husband was in an explosive phase, but she was more concerned with her children's safety than with her own. Later that evening, frantic because her husband had failed to return one of their sons, Raffesberger called a state representative she'd become friends with to ask for advice. While she was on the phone, the front door crashed open and her husband began shooting. Raffesberger ran into her backyard and scaled a seven-foot wooden fence. Just as she reached the top, a bullet grazed her arm and she fell to the other side. Her husband then fired through the fence. A second bullet entered her back, near her spine, shattering five ribs. He used his last bullet on himself, putting the gun to his chest and killing himself. The first squad car on the scene was driven by the policeman who just an hour earlier had spoken with Raffesberger's husband regarding the whereabouts of the son.

Raffesberger has recovered from her physical wounds. Like others whose lives have been profoundly altered by domestic violence, she has chosen to devote her future to working on behalf of other victims. Already her testimony before the Minnesota Legislature has influenced a provision in the federal crime bill that, if enforced, will prohibit the sale of firearms to a man with a valid protection order against him. Raffesberger plans to enter graduate school to study public policy.

Although domestic violence discriminates along gender lines rather than class lines, professional women have one advantage over poor women: their job skills and education. It is precisely because they have independent incomes, says Stark, that some white-collar women are able to extricate themselves.

Still, any advantages women of means may have over poor and blue-collar women are minimal, says Carol Arthur. "White-collar women are like all other women in terms of getting sucked into the psychological and emotional abuse that traps them," she says. "All the messages we got growing up taught us to define ourselves in terms of our relationships." In the end, having the emotional strength to leave that notion behind is what really sets one woman apart from another.

4

Domestic Violence Is a Serious Problem for Black Women

Shawn Sullivan

Shawn Sullivan has been an intern at the Wall Street Journal *and works in New York City.*

The culture of the inner city puts black women at an especially serious risk for domestic violence. The breakdown of families, the pervasive violence that accompanies the drug trade, and misogynistic attitudes (reinforced by rap music lyrics) all contribute to the problem. Encouraging strong, intact families would go far in limiting the abuse of inner-city women by their male partners.

All five of my sisters have been victims of wife-beating. I suppose one could argue that they did not do a good job at selecting their spouses. My sisters live in poor neighborhoods, though, where their kind of bad luck in romance is not out of the ordinary.

In fact, domestic violence may well prove to be the most troubling issue facing poor, urban minority communities for a long time to come. Wife-beating, of course, is not confined to the inner city—it is a national phenomenon. Approximately four million American women are beaten in their homes each year. Wife-beating is the leading cause of emergency-room visits by women, prompting the past two surgeons general to declare it a "medical epidemic."

Many social workers contend that wife-beating in the inner city is not different in intensity or scope from what it is in the society at large. Many of them consider domestic violence to be a manifestation of male sexism and gender dominance in all areas of American society.

My own experiences have shown me that the domestic violence problem is in fact far more complicated. I grew up in Brooklyn's Bedford-Stuyvesant section, one of the poorest neighborhoods in New York City. The atmosphere in a neighborhood like this one fosters a very vicious form of domestic violence.

Women as 'ho's'

Specifically, I mean an atmosphere in which young men are "taught" by their fathers, if they have one, and older brothers to refer to women as "ho's" ("whores") who need abuse; where physical violence is a common means of ending verbal disputes; and where women are mistrusted and detested.

Moral leadership—from within—is what is most needed to combat this environment. Change might begin through political leaders, but families must perpetuate it through radical change in moral training.

This sort of change does not appear to be coming from the social-work establishment. Lucy Friedman, executive director of Victim Services in New York City, the nation's largest domestic-violence agency, does not believe that it is useful to compare the magnitude of the domestic vio-lence problem in different spheres of our society. However, she admits: "Our agency sees more poor people than middle-class and affluent people for domestic violence." By the same token, she quickly adds, there is no reliable statistical basis for asserting that domestic violence is more com-mon in the inner city than in the general society.

This is true. But statistics are so sparse that it is impossible to make a definitive claim on either side of the question. The absence of firm statis-tics, however, does not diminish the undeniable reality that inner-city culture places black women in a very precarious position.

Recently I visited a counseling group for men who had been arrested for wife-beating. John Aponte, the founder of the Alternative to Violence program affiliated with Victim Services, was conducting a workshop with more than 50 alleged wife-beaters in a municipal court building in down-town Brooklyn. Approximately three-quarters of the men were black, 15% Hispanic and 10% white. Virtually all the men lived in urban neigh-borhoods.

Most of the young black batterers at this meeting chose to express their ideas in the style and manner that the inner-city culture fosters. One batterer in his 20s chose to describe his situation to me using the misog-ynistic rhetoric of rap musicians. He admitted hitting his girlfriend but he added: "She simply drove me to frustration. Where I come from, you don't take that s--- from your girl."

Another batterer explained that the way he treated his girlfriend was no different from the way his father treated his mother. He saw nothing particularly wrong with fighting with his girlfriend every so often, even though he is physically stronger. "Yo, man, I do what I can. I have three or four ho's because you don't know what's going to happen tomorrow. They can be sneaky." This extreme distrust of women, and belief in phys-ical violence as the solution to familial disputes, is commonplace among all too many inner-city young men.

Like Ice Cube in the popular movie *Boyz N the Hood*, most young men from the inner city commonly refer to women as "bitches." Rap songs by musicians like Niggaz with Attitudes and Ice Cube glorify date rape and spouse battery. Ice Cube, in particular, defines the essence of this social philosophy in a song called "Steady Mobbing." In this song, he declares, "Life ain't nothing but money and f---ing your bitch."

Ice Cube's album debuted at number one on Billboard's album charts.

His albums, as well as those by Dr. Dre, Cypress Hill and Getto Boys, are bought by millions of young men. All these rap artists paint a picture of a world in which the only important aspect of life is the accumulation of money and the sexual subjugation of women.

Beyond this, their value systems do not go. These are young men who themselves are likely to come from female-headed single-parent homes. Many have never had an older male figure in their family who could be there in times of crisis. They have grown up in communities that have devalued many of the institutions that sustained them in the past—schools, churches and families. Most important, everything they see in their communities—especially from the drug dealers and gang members who control the streets—points to violence as the most suitable recourse for solving their problems.

Domestic violence may well prove to be the most troubling issue facing poor, urban minority communities for a long time to come.

Recently, the Reverend Calvin Butts, of Harlem's Abyssinian Baptist Church, protested the antiwomen lyrics of many rap songs. Although he acknowledges that these rap artists have the right to sing about whatever they like, Mr. Butts believes that pressure—including boycotts—should be placed on record companies to restrict the production of songs like "One Less Bitch," by the group NWA, in which they describe killing women after having sex with them.

"I think that there is a connection between the domestic-violence problem and rap music," says Mr. Butts, "because some songs glorify the horrible things which rappers may have experienced. People who hear this may get the wrong message and think that this behavior is proper." Mr. Butts wants new legislation to restrict sales of such songs.

Regulation is not likely to do much good, however. The problem we are seeing in the inner cities is a deep cultural, and philosophical, one. For example, when I asked a teenage gang member why he feels the need to beat up other people, he said: "Because I can. Why not?" The tragedy here is that there are few, if any, people who are there to give him a satisfactory answer to his question. Unfortunately, the current moral creed seems to be: If you can get away with it, do it.

Republicans have addressed this moral vacuum most directly, but rarely does their rhetoric go beyond demagoguery. Most Democrats, on the other hand, seem to lack the nerve to make categorical moral claims. Cornel West, chairman of the Afro-American studies department at Princeton University, writes in his new bestseller *Race Matters*: "If there is a hidden taboo among liberals, it is to resist talking about values too much because it takes the focus away from structures, especially the positive role of government." Yet if the War on Poverty showed us anything, it is that many government programs have actually contributed to inner-city desolation.

Ms. Friedman of Victim Services and her colleagues are convinced that the government must fund domestic-violence programs in all public schools. It is their belief that the government must become parent and guardian to all those in need of one. But seeing the way things work in Bed-Stuy, I believe that what is most needed is a call for stronger family values. At the core of this problem is the need for parents to demonstrate to their offspring acceptable alternatives to physical violence. It is up to each family to carry out the interchange that would make moral principles a part of daily lives. But it is also abundantly clear that politicians can no longer shirk their responsibility as moral exemplars for their constituencies.

Nihilism is the belief that there is no basis for truth or morality. In *Race Matters*, Mr. West demonstrates how this idea is relevant to the urban condition. Nihilism in the inner city, Mr. West writes, "breeds a cold-hearted, mean-spirited outlook that destroys both the individual and others." It is very clear that those who will be "destroyed" most quickly are young, poor women like my sisters.

5

The Justice System Should Take Domestic Violence More Seriously

Ann Jones

Ann Jones is the author of Women Who Kill *and* Next Time, She'll Be Dead.

From the police's responding to calls to judges' deciding cases at all levels of the courts, the justice system in the United States treats assaults on women by their intimate partners as unimportant. Women who ask for help from police and the courts seldom receive it and, as a result, often are killed by the men who abuse them. The criminal justice system should treat perpetrators of domestic violence as it does others criminals: Batterers should be arrested, prosecuted, and jailed.

Pamela Guenther of Northglenn, Colorado, was 15 when she married her husband, David, and for the better part of the next fifteen years she spoke of leaving him. According to friends interviewed for a documentary on *Frontline*, a public-television news program, Pamela always tried to "smile and be bubbly and to make you feel good," while her husband was a temperamental, surly man who couldn't hold a job and often called the police to complain about his neighbors. One friend said that David threatened to kill Pamela if she ever tried to leave him; another said he was "terribly jealous." Pamela went to work in a doughnut shop to support him and their two children and, said the friends, the couple lived "very quiet lives" at home.

In 1986, after the Guenthers had been married for fourteen years, some partying neighbors went to the Guenther house to harass them. David shot a woman and two men; the woman died of her wounds. At trial, David argued that he had been defending his wife and his property. A judge ruled that under Colorado law, David was within his rights and dismissed the charges against him.

Several months later, Pamela told a friend that David had beaten their son, and she went into hiding with the children. But David sought her out at her job, assaulted her and tried to abduct her. Police charged him with only an incidental matter—failure to report the minor motor-vehicle collision that occurred during the struggle—and let him go.

Pamela quit her job and found another where she wouldn't have to work alone. Her former boss, who had become her boyfriend and given the family shelter, told police David had phoned him and threatened to come after him and Pamela with a gun. Pamela received threatening letters from David, which she turned over to the police. She got a restraining order that evicted David from the family home and restored it to her and the children.

Two days later David forced his way in and held Pamela at gunpoint, ranting about murder. Police surrounded the house, but David held them off for five hours using Pamela as a hostage until she persuaded him to surrender. The police charged him with burglary, and court set bail at $10,000. Within eight hours he had paid the $1,000 required to go free.

David had told an investigating police officer that he was "sorry" and that he had only wanted to talk with his wife. Asked later by *Frontline* if he believed David's story, the police officer said he'd had "no reason not to." On the other hand, a women's-shelter counselor told *Frontline* Pamela said that one of the officers had told her she "was acting awfully calm" for someone who "had been through as much as she claimed." Another counselor said Pamela told her that when she called the police station afterward about David's violation of the restraining order, "the response was, 'Well, that's a civil matter. You have to handle that with your own lawyers.'"

The next day David bought another gun, using Pamela's credit card, and a week later, March 1, 1987, in the parking lot of a restaurant where she and her boyfriend had taken the children to dinner, he shot and killed her. Her boyfriend, shot four times, survived. On March 25, 1988, David Guenthar was convicted of first degree murder and first degree assault. He will be eligible for parole in 2032.

You're not protected

In 1989, the National Commission Against Domestic Violence calculated that a man beat a woman every fifteen seconds; now, they say it's every twelve seconds. And every day women die. Stories like Pamela Guenther's make absorbing TV movies, and the reports always "shock and sadden" press and public alike. Often some official board investigates, some official report is issued, some official wrist is slapped. Some policy is remanded to a committee for further study, and some bereaved relative explains to reporters that the murder victim *did* call the police, she *did* get an order of protection, she *did* leave the man, and yes, she *did* say over and over that he was trying to kill her.

But somebody messed up. Somebody—often *everybody*—in the criminal justice system discounted the woman's complaint, believed the account of the man who terrorized her, and wrote off the criminal assault *as if it had not occurred*. Because the man was dangerous only to her, the law acted as if he weren't dangerous at all.

As Americans, we believe that we possess certain fundamental, inalienable rights, and we count freedom from bodily harm among them. This right underlies all our laws against physical assault, providing their moral foundation. We cede to authorities the right to defend ourselves, and we expect, in return, that they will protect us.

Yet astounding as it may seem, in recent domestic abuse cases in the United States, the courts have chosen not to uphold women's right to freedom from bodily harm, stating that the law is in fact only obligated to protect citizens from being harmed by the state, not from "private violence," i.e., the harm people do to one another. From the standpoint of women and children—who are by far the most common targets of private violence—this legal perspective is inappropriate, and cruelly so. The result: In *theory*, freedom from bodily harm is the right of citizens of this country, but in practice the law does not affirm this right for women.

Instead of safeguarding a woman's right to be free from bodily harm, the law itself *does* her harm. In cases of battering, the courts preserve male privilege by asserting a man's rights to a couple's children or home, by turning a deaf ear to her complaints, by providing "remedies" (such as mediation) that are at best inappropriate, and by generally declining to treat as a crime the kind of physical assault that is in fact a crime on the books of every state.

And while the law no longer suggests that women have *no* right to be free from bodily harm (as it did when a woman was considered the property of her husband and could be disciplined at his discretion), in the peculiar ways it contrives to avoid punishing women's assailants, it continues to enforce that ancient policy. In case after disastrous case, the law is deeply implicated in battering the battered woman.

In recent domestic abuse cases in the United States, the courts have chosen not to uphold women's right to freedom from bodily harm.

The law cannot remedy a woman's complaints because it cannot comprehend them. In any conflict, the law casts the parties as adversaries, but conflict between parties who share a household and/or children is never that simple. A battered woman may want her husband arrested to deter him from beating her again, but if feeding the children depends upon his wages, she may not want him jailed or even prosecuted. On the other hand, if a battered woman does want her assailant locked up forever, as many do, the court is certain to remind her that the man is her husband. In either case, the prosecutor is likely to say that she's wasting the court's time, and the judge may admonish *her* instead of her assaultive husband.

Until quite recently, the law did not even acknowledge that family members might have competing interests. Traditionally, the law assumed that the interests of the paterfamilias and the interests of the family were the same. And even now, the law commonly takes the rights of the husband and father to be "clearly established" rights, taking precedence over the rights of the wife and children. For example, the law is reluctant to evict an assaultive husband from the family home because a man has the right to enjoy "his" home as "his" castle, even when it is the scene of his crimes. (Hence the great need for shelters to house women and children who flee "his" home. Since the criminal is not jailed, the victims must lock *themselves* away; the shelter becomes a jail for crime victims.)

In a great many jurisdictions today, a domestic assault is not treated by the authorities as a real assault. The complaints of a battered woman are typically shunted into municipal or family courts to be heard by civil judges—which often makes the offense complained of *by definition* a civil matter and not a crime. The family-court proceeding, by its very nature, suggests that what has happened is not all that bad. In some jurisdictions *all* battering cases go to family court, so men alleged to have committed felonious assault, or even attempted murder, may evade criminal prosecution altogether. Thus, the state magically transforms the crime into a noncrime.

The practice of bringing assault cases to civil courts may also place women at greater risk because civil-court judges do not receive and review, as a matter of course, the criminal records of men who come before them. In Brookline, Massachusetts, on May 12, 1992, for example, municipal-court judge Lawrence Shubow granted 21-year-old Kristin Lardner the temporary restraining order she sought against ex-boyfriend Michael Cartier. And on May 19, District Judge Paul McGill extended the order for a year. Before the month was out, however, Cartier gunned down Lardner in the street and then killed himself.

As presiding judges in civil proceedings, neither Shubow nor McGill had known that Cartier had a criminal record later described by the *Boston Globe* as "lengthy and bizarre . . . especially against women." Nor did they know that Cartier was on probation, subject to a stayed six-month jail term for attempting to slash a previous girlfriend with scissors. After Kristin Lardner was murdered, Judge Shubow said he was sorry that he had not reviewed Cartier's criminal record. Samuel Zoll, chief justice of the Massachusetts district courts, pointed out that under Massachusetts law at the time, you couldn't "mix civil and criminal records." In September 1992, partly as a result of the Lardner case, Massachusetts passed a law creating a statewide domestic-violence recordkeeping system that includes both civil and criminal records. Judges are now required to consult this information file when considering an application for a restraining or a protective order.

Often judges abdicate responsibility by passing "domestic" assault cases to court-appointed mediators for resolution. For battered women, though, mediation is just as inappropriate as an adversarial contest or a civil proceeding. Like the family-court hearing, mediation suggests that the matter at hand—a criminal assault—is not very important. And like civil-court proceedings, it may place women at greater risk.

Whose responsibility?

Increasingly, endangered women are turning to the courts for protection, encouraged to believe that their best hope for safety lies in the law. But the system is so haphazard, and the judgment of many who administer it so skewed by sympathy for men, that protective procedures often break down. In 1991, 37,000 restraining orders were issued to battered women in Massachusetts alone, yet the death toll of women possessing such orders has continued to rise.

In April 1992, for example, Juan Torres of Lawrence, Massachusetts, shot and killed his common-law wife, Delfina DeLeon, and two of her teenage friends before killing himself. Prior to her death, DeLeon had filed a long series of complaints with the police. She had left Torres, but he broke into her home at least twice and raped her. In March, in violation of a restraining order, he broke in, tied her up with telephone cord, put a gun to her head and according to her father said, "This is the second time. The third time you will die." A warrant was issued for his arrest, and the next day he appeared unexpectedly in court with a lawyer to turn himself in. But no one appeared to give information against him. Neither DeLeon, nor her legal advocate, nor the investigating police officer (who believed that Torres presented an "immediate danger") had been notified of the arraignment. The prosecutor, who had not read the police report or talked to the investigating officer, advised that no bail was necessary. The judge scheduled a hearing in April and released Torres on his own recognizance. Ten days later, after Torres killed DeLeon, the judge said he couldn't recall the case. But he told reporters: "Our capacity to forecast, to predict dangerousness, is imperfect and inexact. You just make the calls, and some of them unfortunately have tragic consequences."

> *The law cannot remedy a woman's complaints because it cannot comprehend them.*

Just as law enforcement has not held batterers to account, most courts have chosen not to hold the police accountable for their refusal to protect women. Battered women have tried suing police departments and municipalities for perceived violations of their constitutional rights, but the more they have pressed for enforcement of laws against assault, the more they have come up against the system that administers and enforces it.

The case of Tracey Thurman is an exception. In 1984 she sued the City of Torrington, Connecticut, and 24 of its police officers for their failure to arrest her violent husband, Charles "Buck" Thurman. He had repeatedly assaulted and attempted to kill her, inflicting permanent injuries. Tracey Thurman claimed a violation of her constitutional rights as set forth in various constitutional amendments, chiefly the Fourteenth, which says, in part, "nor shall any State deprive any person of life, liberty, or property without due process of law; nor deny to any person within its jurisdiction the equal protection of the laws."

Tracey Thurman alleged that by following a policy of not arresting assaultive husbands or boyfriends, Torrington police failed to provide the same protection for abused wives and children as they provided for victims of similar assaults outside a domestic relationship. In a landmark decision, the court agreed, ruling that officers could indeed be held accountable for violating the rights of battered women, and it awarded Tracey Thurman $2.3 million in compensatory damages. Quickly, Connecticut adopted a more comprehensive domestic-violence law, and in the twelve months after it took effect, the number of arrests for domestic assaults increased by 92 percent.

But since then, most courts have taken a different view and ruled against women. For example, when Nancy Watson sued the city of Kansas City, Kansas, her assaultive husband was already dead by his own hand. After he forced his way into her home in January 1984 and raped, beat, and stabbed her, she escaped through a picture window. Ed Watson, a police officer, fled and then killed himself.

In a deposition, Nancy Watson testified that not only had the police previously declined to arrest or discipline Ed Watson, despite Nancy's complaints, but Ed's captain had threatened that if she called the police again he would arrest her and see to it that she lost custody of her two children.

After Ed's death, Nancy Watson filed suit claiming, as Tracey Thurman had, that the police had violated domestic-assault victims' rights to equal protection. Citing Kansas City police records, she pointed out in her lawsuit that during an eight-month period in 1983, 31 percent of the perpetrators in nondomestic assaults were arrested; in domestic assaults, only 16 percent were arrested. In addition, she said, this policy discriminated against women (presumably because women constitute up to 95 percent of the victims of domestic assault).

In some jurisdictions, all *battering cases go to family court, so men alleged to have committed felonious assault, or even attempted murder, may evade criminal prosecution altogether.*

The district court ruled in favor of the city and police on every score, but an appeals court reversed part of the decision. Watson could proceed with her claim, the higher court said, because she had enough evidence to show that the police policy on nonarrest in domestic assault cases resulted in her being treated "differently." But, the court continued, Watson "had failed to present *any* evidence . . . that a policy which discriminates against victims of domestic violence adversely affects women." Even if Watson could prove that, the court said, she also would have to prove that the police "*purposefully*" adopted the policy to discriminate against women.

In subsequent cases like this, the law fashioned even more obstacles for battered women seeking their constitutional rights. And by the time a movie of Tracey Thurman's story reached the television screen in 1989, the U.S. Supreme Court had once and for all snatched the legal rug from under her victory with a landmark ruling in a child-abuse case.

On February 6, 1985, Randy DeShaney, a Wisconsin man, was convicted of felony battery after he beat his 4-year-old son, Joshua, into a coma. A few months later, Joshua's mother, Melody DeShaney, brought suit on her son's behalf against the Winnebago County social services department for violation of Joshua's Fourteenth Amendment rights. In her suit she alleged that the Department of Social Services knowingly left Joshua in the care of his father (her ex-husband) even after the child had repeatedly been observed to have abuse-related injuries. She alleged that Social Services had "deprived Joshua of his liberty without due process of law . . . by failing to intervene to protect him against a risk of violence at his father's hands of which they knew or should have known."

The Supreme Court ruled, in February 1989, that the purpose of the Due Process Clause of the Fourteenth Amendment was "to protect the people from the State, not to ensure that the State protected them from each other." Therefore, the State's "failure to protect an individual against private violence does not constitute a violation" of due process.

Joshua DeShaney's claim was based only on due process, not equal protection, as Tracey Thurman's had been. But in later cases the *DeShaney* decision would be used to block the claims of battered women brought under *either* provision of the Fourteenth Amendment.

Increasingly, endangered women are turning to the courts for protection, encouraged to believe that their best hope for safety lies in the law.

Gayla McKee of Rockwall, Texas, called the police one night in April 1986. She claimed that her live-in boyfriend, Harry Streetman, had assaulted and threatened to kill her. In a later lawsuit against the city, McKee claimed that the two policemen who responded to the call refused to arrest Streetman and refused her request that they take her to the station to file a complaint. According to her suit, one cop told her that she was "inappropriately dressed." Instead, one of them drove her to another apartment, 50 yards away, and left. From there, she telephoned her parents, but while she waited for them, Streetman tracked her down and attacked her with a knife, slashing her right leg.

Gayla McKee sued the individual police officers and the City of Rockwall, claiming "that she had been injured as a result of the officers' refusal to make and arrest, and that this nonarrest was the result of a Rockwall policy that discriminated on the basis of gender." The whole issue of discrimination came to rest on a question of whether the officers involved in the incident had probable cause to make an arrest. In their affidavits, the officers claimed that they had seen no physical evidence that Streetman had beaten her—no "welt, bruise, abrasion, skin discoloration, unneat appearance or any other indication" of assault on Gayla McKee. Besides, the policemen claimed in their affidavits, by the time they arrived, McKee was safely *outside* her apartment (apparently, it didn't occur to them that a woman is entitled to be safely *inside* her home). And the officers claimed "that McKee looked angry rather than hurt, and that Streetman was calm."

The only other evidence the officers had was McKee's word, and it seems clear from the testimony that they did not believe her. McKee claimed that they told her she was exaggerating, suggested she talk things over with Streetman, and told her that "after she had calmed down she probably would not want to file a complaint." McKee claimed that when Streetman threatened—in the presence of the police—to "burn her belongings" if she went to the station, the officers "did not respond in any way." This threat alone would be grounds for arrest, but one police officer claimed in his affidavit that Streetman had made no such threat in his presence.

In short, the officers did what police often do when called to the scene of a "domestic disturbance," and their behavior makes clear that when sex-biased officers look for probable cause for arresting a batterer, no matter how it is defined by statute, they probably won't find it. Even after Streetman tracked McKee down and slashed her with a knife (an incident that one might think would cause the officers to reconsider), they continued to blame McKee. In court, when the city and officers moved to have her claims against them dismissed, they contended that Gayla McKee "was the proximate cause of her own harm."

This is precisely the sort of discriminatory practice, based on prejudice, that the Fourteenth Amendment was designed to redress. Battered women have complained all along that officer "discretion" is a convenient excuse for discrimination. All too often in domestic assaults, police do *not* exercise discretion to evaluate a particular incident. Instead, they routinely refuse to arrest men who assault "their own" women and then chalk up that reaction to discretion. Police "discretion," in other words, is not simply an excuse for discrimination. As it is often exercised, it *is* discrimination.

But not anymore—thanks to the McKee court. The majority's preoccupation with probable cause, as it turned out, was merely a red herring. In the end, the court dismissed all charges against the officers and ruled that even if Gayla McKee could prove that the police had probable cause to arrest Harry Streetman, she *still* couldn't win. Dragging in the *DeShaney* decision, the court reasoned this way: "[The fact] that law enforcement officers have authority to act does not imply that they have any constitutional duty to act." In other words, even if the officers *have* probable cause to make an arrest, they don't have to do so.

Just as law enforcement has not held batterers to account, most courts have chosen not to hold the police accountable for their refusal to protect women.

So much for those of us who believe that the law could and should protect women and redress violations of our constitutional rights. Who is to hold the courts accountable when they enunciate the fundamental biases of an ancient patriarchy? If the police are not required to protect women from bodily harm, if orders of protection are merely pieces of paper, if the courts at every level exist simply to deny what we thought were our rights, then what are we to do? For many battered women, all that remains are the traditional remedies of the noncitizen, the alien or the slave: running away, hiding, or killing the oppressor.

What's needed, then, is to change laws to make them inclusive of women and other marginalized Americans. Currently, feminist legal scholars are working to map alternative routes to securing women's right to be free from bodily harm. Among numerous proposed strategies are these: Suing municipalities for their failure to train public officials properly; pressing for changes in the law rather than money or damages, in the hope that municipalities will negotiate settlements if they are required only to change procedures rather than hand over cash; and pressing for revision of state laws and statutes so that their language clearly establishes the duties of civic officials and creates entitlements of which women cannot be deprived without due process.

None of this will be fast or easy. To hold a municipality liable for failing to train its police to arrest batterers, for example, a woman must prove, among many other things, that the municipality failed to train its police because of "deliberate indifference" to the rights of the public. In addition, proposed federal legislation that aims to combat violence against women has already been whittled down to conform to the strictures of the Supreme Court's ruling in *DeShaney* that the state is not obliged to protect people from each other. Title III of the Violence Against Women Act, a bill that was first proposed in 1990 and was scheduled for a Senate vote by the end of 1993, would provide a civil rights remedy for violent, gender-based discrimination—but only up to a point. It still will not permit claims "that a government entity has violated a citizen's due process rights by failing to protect him or her."

One has to ask: Should it be *this* hard to claim in court a constitutional protection so basic that most white men don't ever have to think about it? We must profoundly change the way the law is interpreted, applied and enforced.

And that would seem to hinge upon a transformation of consciousness. Just as our consciousness of rape was raised in the 1980s, our consciousness of assault and battery must now be raised. We've learned that any social, economic or political development that counteracts sexism and promotes sex equality helps in the long run to eliminate violence by reducing the *power* men hold, institutionally and individually, over women. But in the short run, the single most effective way to protect women, save lives and cut down violence is to treat assault as the crime it is: Arrest batterers and send them to jail.

6

Domestic Violence Is a Problem for Men

Murray A. Straus

Murray A. Straus is the director of the Center on Family Violence at the University of New Hampshire in Durham and a well-known researcher and author on domestic violence.

Long-term research has revealed that women and men are equally likely to be the physical aggressors in domestic conflicts. Contrary to stereotypes, men are actually more likely than women to be victims of spousal abuse, although women receive more serious injuries. Men deserve the same compassion and support as female victims of domestic violence.

The first purpose of this viewpoint is to review research that shows that women initiate and carry out physical assaults on their partners as often as men do. A second purpose is to show that, despite the much lower probability of physical injury resulting from attacks by women, assaults by women are a serious social problem, just as it would be if men "only" slapped their wives or "only" slapped female fellow employees and produced no injury. One of the main reasons "minor" assaults by women are such an important problem is that they put women in danger of much more severe retaliation by men. They also help perpetuate the implicit cultural norms that make the marriage license a hitting license. It will be argued that, to end "wife beating," it is essential for women also to end the seemingly "harmless" pattern of slapping, kicking, or throwing things at male partners who persist in some outrageous behavior and "won't listen to reason."

The viewpoint focuses exclusively on physical assaults, even though they are not necessarily the most damaging type of abuse. One can hurt a partner deeply—even drive the person to suicide—without ever lifting a finger. Verbal aggression may be even more damaging than physical attacks (Vissing, Straus, Gelles, and Harrop, 1991). This viewpoint is concerned only with physical assaults because, with rare exception, the controversy has been about "violence," that is, physical assaults, by wives.

The National Crime Panel Report defines *assault* as "an unlawful physical attack by one person upon another" (U.S. Department of Justice, 1976). It is important to note that neither this definition nor the definition used for reporting assaults to the Federal Bureau of Investigation (1989) requires injury or bodily contact. Thus if a person is chased by someone attempting to hit the individual with a stick or to stab the person, and the victim escapes, the attack is still a felony-level crime—an "aggravated assault"—even though the victim was not touched. Nevertheless, in the real world, the occurrence of an injury makes a difference in what the police, prosecutors, and juries do. Consequently, injury will also be considered in this viewpoint.

Gender differences in spouse assault and homicide rates

The National Family Violence Surveys obtained data from nationally representative samples of 2,143 married and cohabiting couples in 1975 and 6,002 couples in 1985 (information on the sample and methodology is given in Gelles and Straus, 1988; Straus and Gelles, 1986, 1990). Previously published findings have shown that, in both surveys, the rate of wife-to-husband assault was about the same (actually slightly higher) than the husband-to-wife assault rate (Straus and Gelles, 1986, 1990). However, the seeming equality may occur because of a tendency by husbands to underreport their own assaults (Dutton, 1988; Edleson and Brygger, 1986; Jouriles and O'Leary, 1985; Stets and Straus, 1990; Szinovacz, 1983). To avoid the problem of male underreporting, the assault rates were recomputed for this viewpoint on the basis of information provided by the 2,994 women in the 1985 National Family Violence Survey. The resulting overall rate for assaults by wives is 124 per 1,000 couples, compared with 122 per 1,000 for assaults by husbands *as reported by wives*. This difference is not great enough to be statistically significant. Separate rates were also computed for minor and severe assaults. The rate of minor assaults by wives was 78 per 1,000 couples, and the rate of minor assaults by husbands was 72 per 1,000. The severe assault rate was 46 per 1,000 couples for assaults by wives and 50 per 1,000 for assaults by husbands. Neither difference is statistically significant. As these rates are based exclusively on information provided by women respondents, the near equality in assault rates cannot be attributed to a gender bias in reporting.

> *Women initiate and carry out physical assaults on their partners as often as men do.*

As pointed out elsewhere, female assault rates based on the Conflict Tactics Scales (CTS) can be misleading because the CTS does not measure the purpose of the violence, such as whether it is in self-defense, nor does it measure injuries resulting from assaults (Straus, 1977, 1980; Straus, Gelles, and Steinmetz, 1980). That information must be obtained by additional questions, and the 1985 National Family Violence Survey included questions on who initiated violence and questions on injuries.

Injury adjusted rates Stets and Straus (1990) and Brush (1990) provide data that can be used to adjust the rates to take into account whether the assault resulted in an injury. Stets and Straus found a rate of 3% for injury-producing assaults by men and 0.4% for injury-producing assaults by women. Somewhat lower injury rates were found by Brush for another large national sample—1.2% of injury-producing assaults by men and 0.2% for injury-producing assaults by women. An "injury adjusted" rate was computed using the higher of the two injury estimates. The resulting rate of injury-producing assaults by husbands is 3.7 per 1,000 (122 x .03 = 3.66), and the rate of injury-producing assaults by wives is much lower—0.5 per 1,000 (124 x .004 = 0.49). Thus the injury adjusted rate for assaults by men is seven times greater than the rate of domestic assaults by women.

Although the injury adjusted rates correspond more closely to police and National Crime Victimization Survey statistics (see below), there are several disadvantages to rates based on injury (Straus, 1990, pp. 79–83), two of which will be mentioned. One of the disadvantages is that the criterion of injury contradicts the new domestic assault legislation and new police policies. These statutes and policies premise restraining orders and encourage arrest on the basis of attacks. They do not require observable injury.

Another disadvantage of using injury as a criterion for domestic assault is that injury-based rates omit the 97% of assaults by husbands that do not result in injury but that are nonetheless a serious social problem. Without an adjustment for injury, the National Family Violence Survey produces an estimate of more than 6 million women assaulted by a male partner each year, of which 1.8 million are "severe" assaults (Straus and Gelles, 1990). If the injury adjusted rate is used, the estimate is reduced to 188,000 assaulted women per year. The figure of 1.8 million seriously assaulted women every year has been used in many legislative hearings and countless feminist publications to indicate the prevalence of the problem. If that estimate had to be replaced by 188,000, it would understate the extent of the problem and could handicap efforts to educate the public and secure funding for shelters and other services. Fortunately, that is not necessary. Both estimates can be used, because they highlight different aspects of the problem.

Other surveys of married and dating couples

Married and cohabiting couples Although there may be exceptions that I missed, *every* study among the more than 30 describing some type of sample that is not self-selective (such as community random samples and samples of college student dating couples) has found a rate of assault by women on male partners that is about the same as the rate of assault by men on female partners. The space available does not permit me to describe each of those studies, but they include research by respected scholars such as Scanzoni (1978) and Tyree and Malone (1991) and large-scale studies such as the Los Angeles Epidemiology Catchment Area study (Sorenson and Telles, 1991), the National Survey of Households and Families (Brush, 1990), and the survey conducted for the Kentucky Commission on Women (Schulman, 1979).

The Kentucky study also brings out a troublesome question of scientific ethics, because it is one of several in which the data on assaults by women were intentionally suppressed. The existence of those data became known only because Hornung, McCullough, and Sugimoto (1981) obtained the computer tape and found that, among the violent couples, 38% were attacks by women on men who, as reported by the women themselves, had not attacked them. Some of the other studies that found approximately equal rates are cited in Straus and Gelles (1990, pp. 95–105).

The rate of wife-to-husband assault was about the same (actually slightly higher) than the husband-to-wife assault rate.

Dating couples Sugarman and Hotaling (1989) summarize the results of 21 studies that reported gender differences in assault. They found that the average assault rate was 329 per 1,000 for men and 393 per 1,000 for women. Sugarman and Hotaling comment that a "surprising finding . . . is the *higher* proportion of females than males who self-report having expressed violence in a dating relationship" (p. 8; emphasis added). Moreover, other studies published since their review further confirm the high rate of assault by women in dating relationships (see, e.g., Pirog-Good and Stets, 1989; Stets and Straus, 1990).

Samples of "battered women" Studies of residents in shelters for battered women are sometimes cited to show that it is only their male partners who are violent. However, these studies rarely obtain or report information on assaults by women, and when they do, they ask only about self-defense. Pagelow's (1981) questionnaire, for example, presents respondents with a list of "factors responsible for causing the battering," but the list does not include an attack *by* the woman, therefore precluding finding information on female-initiated assaults. One of the few exceptions is in the work of Walker (1984), who found that one out of four women in battering relationships had answered affirmatively that they had "used physical force to get something [they] wanted" (p. 174). Another is the study by Giles-Sims (1983) that found that in the year prior to coming to a shelter, 50% of the women reported assaulting their partners, and in the six months after leaving the shelter, 41.7% reported an assault against a spouse. These assaults could all have been in self-defense, but Giles-Sims's case study data suggest that this is not likely.

Government crime statistics

National Crime Victimization Survey The National Crime Victimization Survey (NCVS) is an annual study of approximately 60,000 households, conducted for the Department of Justice by the Bureau of the Census. Analysis of the NCVS for the period 1973–1975 by Gaquin (1977–1978) found an extremely low rate of marital violence—2.2 per 1,000 couples. By comparison, the 1985 National Family Violence Survey found a rate of 161 per 1,000, which is 73 times higher. The NCVS rate for assaults by husbands is 3.9 per 1,000; the rate is 0.3 for assaults by wives. Thus, according to the NCVS, the rate of domestic assaults by husbands is 13 times greater than the rate of assaults by wives.

The extremely low rates of assaults by both husbands and wives found by the NCVS may be accounted for by the fact that NCVS interviews were conducted with both partners present, and victims may have been reluctant to respond out of fear of further violence. Perhaps even more important, the NCVS is presented to respondents as a study of crime. The difficulty with a "crime survey" as the context for estimating rates of domestic assault is that most people think of being kicked by their partners as wrong, but not a "crime" in the legal sense. It takes relatively rare circumstances, such as an injury or an attack by a former spouse who "has no right to do that," for the attack to be perceived as a "crime" (Langan and Innes, 1986). This is probably why the NCVS produces such totally implausible statistics as a 75% injury rate (compared with an injury rate of less than 3% in the two surveys cited earlier) and more assaults by former partners than by current partners. This is because, in the context of a crime survey, people tend to report attacks only when they have been experienced as "real crimes," because they resulted in injury or were perpetrated by former partners.

Police calls Data on calls for domestic assaults to the police are biased in ways that are similar to the bias of the National Crime Victimization Survey. As in the NCVS, at least 93% of the cases are missed (Kaufman Kantor, and Straus, 1990), probably because there was no injury or threat of serious injury great enough to warrant calling the police. Because the cases for which police are called tend to involve injury or chronic severe assault, and because that tends to be a male pattern, assaults by women are rarely recorded by police. Another reason assaults by women are rare in police statistics is that many men are reluctant to admit that they cannot "handle" their wives. These artifacts produce a rate of assaults by men that is hugely greater than the rate of assaults by women. Dobash and Dobash (1979), for example, found that only 1% of intrafamily assault cases in two Scottish cities were assaults by wives.

Spouse homicide rates

Homicide rates published by the FBI show that only 14% of homicide offenders are women (calculated from Federal Bureau of Investigation, 1989, unnumbered table at bottom of p. 9). However, the percentages of female offenders vary tremendously according to the relationships between offenders and victims. Female-perpetrated homicides of *strangers* occur at a rate that is less than a twentieth the male rate. The female share goes up somewhat for murders of *acquaintances*. As for murders of *family* members, women committed them at a rate that was almost half the rate of men in the period 1976–1979 and more than a third of the male rate during the period 1980–1984.

However, *family* includes all relatives, whereas the main focus of this viewpoint is couples. Two recent gender-specific estimates of the rates for partner homicide indicate that wives murder male partners at a rate that is 56% (Straus, 1986) and 62% (Browne and Williams, 1989) as great as the rate of partner homicides by husbands. This is far from equality but it also indicates that, in partner relationships, even when the assaults are so extreme as to result in death, the rate for wives is extremely high, whereas, as noted above, for murders of strangers the female rate is only a twentieth of the male rate.

Self-defense and assaults by wives

I have explained the high rate of attacks on spouses by wives as largely a *response* to or a defense against assault by the partner (Straus, 1977, 1980; Straus et al., 1980). However, new evidence raises questions about that interpretation.

Homicide For lethal assaults by women, a number of studies suggest that a substantial proportion are self-defense, retaliation, or acts of desperation following years of brutal victimization (Browne, 1987; Browne and Williams, 1989; Jurik, 1989; Jurik and Gregware, 1989). However, Jurik (1989) and Jurik and Gregware's (1989) investigation of 24 cases in which women killed husbands or lovers found that the victim initiated use of physical force in 10 (40%) of the cases. Jurik and Gregware's second table shows that only 5 out of the 24 homicides (21%) were in response to "prior abuse" or "threat of abuse/death." Mann's (1990) study of the circumstances surrounding partner homicides by wives shows that many women who murder their spouses are impulsive, violent, and have criminal records. Jurik (1989) and Jurik and Gregware (1989) also report that 60% of the women they studied had previous arrests. The widely cited study by Wolfgang (1958) refers to "victim-precipitated" homicides, but the case examples indicate that these homicides include cases of retaliation as well as self-defense.

Wife-only violence Of the 495 couples in the 1985 National Family Violence Survey for whom one or more assaultive incidents were reported by a woman respondent, the husband was the only violent partner in 25.9% of the cases, the wife was the only one to be violent in 25.5% of the cases, and both were violent in 48.6% of the cases. Thus a minimum estimate of violence by wives that is *not* self-defense because the wife is the only one to have used violence in the past 12 months is 25%. Brush (1990) reports similar results for the couples in the National Survey of Families and Households.

About as many women as men attacked spouses who had not hit them.

Perhaps the real gender difference occurs in assaults that carry a greater risk of causing physical injury, such as punching, kicking, and attacks with weapons. This hypothesis was investigated using the 211 wives who reported one or more instances of a "severe" assault. The resulting proportions were similar: both, 35.2%; husband only, 35.2%; and wife only, 29.6%.

The findings just reported show that regardless of whether the analysis is based on all assaults or is focused on dangerous assaults, about as many women as men attacked spouses who had *not* hit them during the one-year referent period. This is inconsistent with the self-defense explanation for the high rate of domestic assault by women. However, it is possible that, among the couples where both assaulted, all the women were acting in self-defense. Even if that unlikely assumption were correct, it would still be true that 25–30% of violent marriages are violent solely because of attacks by the wife.

Initiation of attacks The 1985 National Family Violence Survey asked respondents, "Let's talk about the last time you and your partner got into a physical fight and [the most severe act previously mentioned] happened. In that particular instance, who started the physical conflict, you or your partner?" According to the 446 wives involved in violent relationships, their partners struck the first blows in 42.3% of the cases, the women hit first in 53.1% of the cases, and the women could not remember or could not disentangle who hit first in the remaining 3.1% of the cases.

Similar results were obtained by five other studies. Bland and Orne's (1986) study of marital violence and psychiatric disorder in Canada found that wives initiated violence somewhat more often than did husbands. Gryl and Bird (1989) found that "respondents in violent dating relationships indicated that their partners initiated the violence 51% of the time; they initiated it 41% of the time; and both were equally responsible 8% of the time." Saunders (1989) analyzed data on the sequence of events in the 1975 National Family Violence Survey and found that women respondents indicated that they struck the first blow in 40% of the cases. Henton, Cate, Koval, Lloyd, and Christopher (1983) found that "in 48.7% . . . of the relationships, the respondent perceived that both partners were responsible for 'starting' the violence" (p. 472). A large-scale Canadian study found that women struck the first blow about as often as men. However, as in the case of the Kentucky survey mentioned earlier, the authors have not published the findings, perhaps because they are not "politically correct."

Is the high rate of assault by wives explainable as self-defense?

It is remarkable that every study that has investigated who initiates violence using methods that do not preclude the possibility of a wife beating found that wives initiate violence in a large proportion of cases. However, caution is needed in interpreting these findings, for several reasons.

First, some respondents may have answered the question in terms of who began *the argument*, not who began *hitting*. Interviewers were instructed to rephrase the question in such cases. However, there may have been instances in which the misunderstanding of the question went unnoticed.

Second, if the wife hit first, that could still be in self-defense if her attack was in response to a situation that she defined as posing a threat of grave harm from which she could not otherwise escape (Browne, 1987; Jurik, 1989; Jurik and Gregware, 1989).

A third reason for caution is the limited data available in the National Family Violence Survey on the context of the assaults. Who initiates an assault and who is injured are important aspects of the contextual information needed for a full understanding of the gendered aspects of intrafamily assault, but they are not sufficient. For example, there may have been an escalation of assaults throughout the relationship, with the original attacks by the man. The fact that the most recent incident happened to be initiated by the female partner ignores the history and the context producing that act, which may be one of utter terror. This scenario is common in cases of women who kill abusive male partners. A battered woman may kill her partner when he is not attacking her, and thus may appear not to be acting in self-defense. As Browne (1987), Jurik (1989), and Jurik and Gregware (1989) show, the traditional criteria for self-defense use assumptions based on male characteristics that ignore physical size and strength differences between men and women and ignore the economic dependency that locks some women into relationships in which they have legitimate grounds for fearing for their lives.

There seems to be an implicit cultural norm permitting or encouraging minor assaults by wives in certain circumstances.

The scenario described above is often recounted by clients of shelters for battered women. However, it is hazardous to extrapolate from the situation of women in those extreme situations to the pattern of assaults that characterizes couples in the general population as represented in the National Family Violence Survey. This issue is discussed more fully later in this viewpoint, in the section on the representative sample fallacy. For the moment, let us assume that many of the assaults initiated by wives are in response to fear derived from a long prior history of victimization. Even if that is the case, it is a response that tends to elicit further assaults by the male partner (Bowker, 1983; Feld and Straus, 1989; Gelles and Straus, 1988, chap. 7; Straus, 1974).

In the light of these qualifications and cautions, the self-defense explanation of the near equality between husbands and wives in domestic assaults cannot be rejected. However, one can conclude that the research on who hit first does not support the hypothesis that assaults by wives are primarily acts of self-defense or retaliation.

Different kinds of attacks

Although the prevalence rate of assaults by wives is about the same as that for husbands, husbands may engage in more *repeated* attacks. This hypothesis was investigated by computing the mean number of assaults among couples for which at least one assault was reported by a female respondent. According to these 495 women, their partners averaged 7.2 assaults during the year, and they themselves averaged six assaults. Although the frequency of assault by husbands is greater than the frequency of assault by wives, the difference is just short of being statistically significant. If the analysis is restricted to the 165 cases of severe assault, the husbands averaged 6.1 and the wives 4.28 assaults, which is a 42% greater frequency of assault by husbands and is also just short of being statistically significant. If one disregards the tests of statistical significance, these comparisons support the hypothesized greater chronicity of violence by husbands. At the same time, the fact that the average number of assaults by husbands is higher should not obscure the fact that the violent *wives* carried out an average of six minor and five severe assaults per year, indicating a repetitive pattern by wives as well as by husbands. The discrepancy between the findings from surveys of family problems and findings based on criminal justice system data or the experiences of women in shelters for battered women does not indicate that one set of statistics is correct and the other not. Both are correct. However, they apply to different groups of people and reflect different aspects of domestic assault. Most of the violence that is revealed by surveys of family problems is relatively minor and relatively infrequent, whereas most of the violence in official statistics is chronic and severe and involves injuries that need medical attention. These two types of violence probably have different etiologies and probably require different types of intervention. It is important not to use findings based on cases known to the police or shelters for battered women as the basis for deciding how to deal with the relatively minor and infrequent violence found in the population in general. That type of unwarranted generalization is often made; it is known as the *clinical fallacy*.

Representative community sample studies have the opposite problem, which can be called the *representative sample fallacy* (Straus, 1990; see also Gelles, 1991). Community samples contain very few cases involving severe assaults every week or more often and injury. Men tend to be the predominant aggressors in this type of case, but representative sample studies cannot reveal that, because they include few if any such cases. Ironically, the types of cases that are not covered by community surveys are the most horrible cases and the ones that everyone wants to do something about. However, community surveys can tell us little about what to do about these extreme cases because the samples contain too few to analyze separately.

It is painful to have to recognize the high rate of domestic assaults by women.

The controversy over assaults by women largely stems from survey researchers' assumptions that their findings on rates of spouse assault by men and women apply to cases known to the police and to shelters, and the similar unwarranted assumption by clinical researchers that the predominance of assaults by men applies to the population at large.

Both community sample data and clinical sample data are needed. Community sample data are essential for informing programs directed at the larger community, especially programs intended to prevent such cases in the first place or to prevent them from developing into "clinical cases." Conversely, it is essential to have research on clinical samples, such as those involved with the police or shelters for battered women, in order to have data that do apply to such cases and that therefore provide a realistic basis for programs designed to aid the victims and to end the most serious type of domestic violence.

The number of assaults by itself, however, ignores the contexts, meanings, and consequences of these assaults. The fact that assaults by women produce far less injury is a critical difference. There are probably other important differences between men and women in assaults on partners. For example, a man may typically hit or threaten to hit to force some specific behavior on pain of injury, whereas a woman may typically slap a partner or pound on his chest as an expression of outrage or in frustration because of his having turned a deaf ear to repeated attempts to discuss some critical issue (Greenblat, 1983). Despite this presumed difference, both are uses of physical violence for coercion.

A meta-analysis of research on gender differences in aggression by Eagly and Steffen (1986) brings out a related difference in context and meaning. These researchers found no *overall* difference in aggression by men and women, but less aggression by women if the act would produce harm to the target. These and other differences in context, meaning, and motivation are important for understanding violence by women against partners, but they do not indicate the absence of assault by women. Nor do differences between men and women in the histories, meanings, objectives, and consequences of assaults refute the hypothesis discussed below: that assaults by wives help legitimate male violence. Only empirical research can resolve that issue.

Violence by wives increases the probability of wife beating

There seems to be an implicit cultural norm permitting or encouraging minor assaults by wives in certain circumstances. Stark and McEvoy (1970) found about equal support for a wife hitting a husband as for a husband hitting a wife. Greenblat (1983) found that both men and women are *more* accepting of wives hitting husbands than of husbands hitting wives. Data from the National Family Violence Survey also show more public acceptance of a wife slapping a husband than of a husband slapping a wife. Greenblat suggests that this is because "female aggressors are far less likely to do physical harm" (p. 247). These norms tolerating low-level violence by women are transmitted and learned in many ways. For example, even casual observation of the mass media suggests that just about every day, there are scenes depicting a man who makes an insulting or outrageous statement and an indignant woman who responds by "slapping the cad," thus presenting an implicit model of assault as a morally correct behavior to millions of women.

Let us assume that most of the assaults by wives fall into the "slap the cad" genre and are not intended to, and only rarely, cause physical injury. The danger to women is shown by studies that find that minor violence by wives increases the probability of severe assaults by husbands (Bowker, 1983; Feld and Straus, 1989; Gelles and Straus, 1988, pp. 146–156). Sometimes this is immediate and severe retaliation. Regardless of whether that occurs, however, a more indirect and probably more important effect may be that such morally correct slapping acts out and reinforces the traditional tolerance of assault in marriage. The moral justification of assault implicit when a woman slaps or throws something at a partner for doing something outrageous reinforces his moral justification for slapping her when *she* is doing something outrageous, or when she is obstinate, nasty, or "not listening to reason" as he sees it. To the extent that this is correct, one of the many steps needed in primary prevention of assaults on wives is for women to forsake even "harmless" physical attacks on male partners and children. Women must insist on nonviolence from their sisters, just as they rightfully insist on it from men.

It is painful to have to recognize the high rate of domestic assaults by women. Moreover, the statistics are likely to be used by misogynists and apologists for male violence. The problem is similar to that noted by Barbara Hart (1986) in the introduction to a book on lesbian battering: "[It] is painful. It challenges our dream of a lesbian utopia. It contradicts our belief in the inherent nonviolence of women. And the disclosure of violence by lesbians . . . may enhance the arsenal of homophobes. . . . Yet, if we are to free ourselves, we must free our sisters" (p. 10). My view of recognizing violence by wives is parallel to Hart's view on lesbian battering. It is painful, but to do otherwise obstructs a potentially important means of reducing assaults by husbands—raising the consciousness of women about the implicit norms that are reinforced by a ritualized slap for outrageous behavior on the part of their partners.

Ending assaults by *wives needs to be added to efforts to prevent assaults* on *wives.*

It follows from the above that efforts to prevent assaults by husbands must include attention to assaults by wives. Although this may seem like "victim blaming," there is an important difference. Recognizing that assaults by wives are one of the many causes of wife beating does not justify such assaults. It is the responsibility of husbands as well as wives to refrain from physical attacks (including retaliation), at home as elsewhere, no matter what the provocation.

Ending assaults *by* wives needs to be added to efforts to prevent assaults *on* wives for a number of reasons. Perhaps the most fundamental reason is the intrinsic moral wrong of assaulting a spouse, as expressed in the fact that such assaults are criminal acts, even when no injury occurs. A second reason is the unintended validation of the traditional cultural norms tolerating a certain level of violence between spouses. A third reason is the danger of escalation when wives engage in "harmless" minor violence. Feld and Straus (1989) found that if the female partner also engaged in an assault, it increased the probability that assaults would persist or escalate in severity over the one-year period of their study, whereas if only one partner engaged in physical attacks, the probability of cessation increased. Finally, assault of a spouse "models" violence for children. This effect is as strong for assaults by wives as it is for assaults by husbands (Jaffe, Wolfe, and Wilson, 1990; Straus, 1983, 1992; Straus et al., 1980).

It should be emphasized that the preventive effect of reducing minor assaults by wives has not been proven by the evidence in this viewpoint. It is a plausible inference and a hypothesis for further research. Especially needed are studies to test the hypothesis that "harmless" assaults by wives strengthen the implicit moral justification for assaults by husbands. If the research confirms that hypothesis, it would indicate the need to add reduction of assaults by wives to efforts to end wife beating, including public service announcements, police arrest policy, and treatment programs for batterers. Such changes must be made with extreme care for a number of reasons, not the least of which is to avoid implying that violence by women justifies or excuses violence by their partners. Moreover, although women may assault their partners at approximately the same rate as men assault theirs, because of the greater physical, financial, and emotional injury suffered, women are the predominant victims (Stets and Straus, 1990; Straus et al., 1980). Consequently, first priority in services for victims and in prevention and control must continue to be directed toward assaults by husbands.

References

Bland, R., and Orne, H. (1986). Family violence and psychiatric disorder. *Canadian Journal of Psychiatry, 31*, 129–137.

Bowker, L. H. (1983). *Beating wife-beating.* Lexington, MA: Lexington.

Browne, A. (1987). *When battered women kill.* New York: Free Press.

Browne, A., and Williams, K. R. (1989). Exploring the effect of resource availability and the likelihood of female-perpetrated homicides. *Law and Society Review, 23* (1), 75–94.

Brush, L. D. (1990). Violent acts and injurious outcomes in married couples: Methodological issues in the National Survey of Families and Households. *Gender & Society, 4*, 56–67.

Dobash, R. E., and Dobash, R. P. (1979). *Violence against wives: A case against the patriarchy.* New York: Free Press.

Dutton, D. G. (1988). *The domestic assault of women: Psychological and criminal justice perspectives.* Boston: Allyn & Bacon.

Eagly, A. H., and Steffen, V. J. (1986). Gender and aggressive behavior: A meta-analytic review of the social psychological literature. *Psychological Bulletin, 100*, 309–330.

Edleson, J. L., and Brygger, M. P. (1986). Gender differences in reporting of battering incidents. *Family Relations, 35*, 377–382.

Federal Bureau of Investigation. (1989). *Crime in the United States.* Washington, DC: U.S. Department of Justice.

Feld, S. L., and Straus, M. A. (1989). Escalation and desistance of wife assault in marriage. *Criminology, 27*, 141–161.

Gaquin, D. A. (1977–1978). Spouse abuse: Data from the National Crime Survey. *Victimology, 2*, 632–642.

Gelles, R. J. (1991). Physical violence, child abuse, and child homicide: A continuum of violence or distinct behaviors? *Human Nature, 2*, 59–72.

Gelles, R. J., and Straus, M. A. (1988). *Intimate violence: The causes and consequences of abuse in the American family.* New York: Simon and Schuster.

Giles-Sims, J. (1983). *Wife battering: A systems theory approach.* New York: Guilford.

Greenblat, C. S. (1983). A hit is a hit is a hit . . . or is it? Approval and tolerance of the use of physical force by spouses. In D. Finkelhor, R. J. Gelles, G. T. Hotaling, and M. A. Straus (Eds.), *The dark side of families: Current family violence research* (pp. 235–260). Beverly Hills, CA: Sage.

Gryl, F. E., and Bird, G. W. (1989). *Close dating relationships among college students: Differences by gender and by use of violence.* Paper presented at the annual meeting of the National Council on Family Relations, New Orleans.

Hart, B. (1986). Preface. In K. Lobel (Ed.), *Naming the violence: Speaking out about lesbian battering* (pp. 9–16). Seattle, WA: Seal.

Henton, J., Cate, R., Koval, J., Lloyd, S., and Christopher, S. (1983). Romance and violence in dating relationships. *Journal of Family Issues, 4,* 467–482.

Hornung, C. A., McCullough, B. C., and Sugimoto, T. (1981). Status relationships in marriage: Risk factors in spouse abuse. *Journal of Marriage and the Family, 43,* 675–692.

Jaffe, P. G., Wolfe, D. A., and Wilson, S. K. (1990). *Children of battered women: Issues in child development and intervention planning.* Newbury Park, CA: Sage.

Jouriles, E. N., and O'Leary, K. D. (1985). Interspousal reliability of reports of marital violence. *Journal of Consulting and Clinical Psychology, 53,* 419–421.

Jurik, N. C. (1989, November). *Women who kill and the reasonable man: The legal issues surrounding female-perpetrated homicide.* Paper presented at the 41st Annual Meeting of the American Society of Criminology, Reno, NV.

Jurik, N. C., and Gregware, P. (1989). *A method for murder: An interactionist analysis of homicides by women.* Tempe: Arizona State University, School of Justice Studies.

Kaufman Kantor, G., and Straus, M. A. (1990). Response of victims and the police to assaults on wives. In M. A. Straus and R. J. Gelles (Eds.), *Physical violence in American families: Risk factors and adaptations to violence in 8,145 families* (pp. 473–486). New Brunswick, NJ: Transaction.

Langan, P. and Innes, C. A. (1986). *Preventing domestic violence against women* (Bureau of Justice Statistics Special Report). Washington, DC: U.S. Department of Justice.

Mann, C. R. (1990). Black female homicide in the United States. *Journal of Interpersonal Violence, 5,* 176–201.

Pagelow, M. D. (1981). *Woman-battering: Victims and their experiences.* Beverly Hills, CA: Sage.

Pirog-Good, M. A., and Stets, J. E. (Eds.). (1989). *Violence in dating relationships: Emerging social issues.* New York: Praeger.

Saunders, D. G. (1989, November). *Who hits first and who hurts most? Evidence for the greater victimization of women in intimate relationships.* Paper presented at the 41st Annual Meeting of the American Society of Criminology, Reno, NV.

Scanzoni, J. (1978). *Sex roles, women's work, and marital conflict.* Lexington, MA: Lexington.

Schulman, M. (1979, July). *A survey of spousal violence against women in Kentucky* (Study No. 792701, conducted for Kentucky Commission on Women, sponsored by the U.S. Department of Justice, Law Enforcement Assistance Administration). Washington, DC: Government Printing Office.

Sorenson, S. B., and Telles, C. A. (1991). Self-reports of spousal violence in a Mexican-American and non-Hispanic white population. *Violence and Victims, 6,* 3–15.

Stark, R., and McEvoy, J., III. (1970, November). Middle class violence. *Psychology Today, 4,* 52–65.

Stets, J. E., and Straus, M. A. (1990). Gender differences in reporting marital violence and its medical and psychological consequences. In M. A. Straus and R. J. Gelles (Eds.), *Physical violence in American families: Risk factors and adaptations to violence in 8,245 families* (pp. 151–166). New Brunswick, NJ: Transaction.

Straus, M. A. (1974). Leveling, civility, and violence in the family. *Journal of Marriage and the Family, 36,* 13–29.

Straus, M. A. (1977, March). Normative and behavioral aspects of violence between spouses: Preliminary data on a nationally representative USA sample. In *Violence in Canadian Society.* Symposium sponsored by Simon Fraser University, Department of Criminology, at the University of New Hampshire Family Research Laboratory, Durham.

Straus, M. A. (1980). Victims and aggressors in marital violence. *American Behavioral Scientist, 23,* 681–704.

Straus, M. A. (1983). Ordinary violence, child abuse, and wife-beating: What do they have in common? In D. Finkelhor, R. J. Gelles, G. T. Hotaling, and M. A. Straus (Eds.), *The dark side of families: Current family violence research* (pp. 213–234). Beverly Hills, CA: Sage.

Straus, M. A. (1986). Domestic violence and homicide antecedents. *Domestic Violence, 62,* 446–465.

Straus, M. A. (1990). Injury and frequency of assault and the "representative sample fallacy" in measuring wife beating and child abuse. In M. A. Straus and R. J. Gelles (Eds.), *Physical violence in American families: Risk factors and adaptations to violence in 8,145 families* (pp. 75–91). New Brunswick, NJ: Transaction.

Straus, M. A. (1992). Children as witnesses to marital violence: A risk factor for lifelong problems among a nationally representative sample of American men and women. In D. F. Schwarz (Ed.), *Children and violence: Report of the Twenty-Third Ross Roundtable on Critical Approaches to Common Pediatric Problems in collaboration with the Ambulatory Pediatric Association.* Columbus, OH: Ross Laboratories.

Straus, M. A., and Gelles, R. J. (1986). Societal change and change in family violence from 1975 to 1985 as revealed by two national surveys. *Journal of Marriage and the Family, 48,* 465–479.

Straus, M. A., and Gelles, R. J. (Eds.). (1990). *Physical violence in American families: Risk factors and adaptations to violence in 8,245 families.* New Brunswick, NJ: Transaction.

Straus, M. A., Gelles, R. J., and Steinmetz, S. K. (1980). *Behind closed doors: Violence in the American family.* Garden City, NY: Anchor/Doubleday.

Sugarman, D. B., and Hotaling, G. T. (1989). Dating violence: Prevalence, context, and risk markers. In M. A. Pirog-Good and J. E. Stets (Eds.), *Violence in dating relationships: Emerging social issues.* New York: Praeger.

Szinovacz, M. E. (1983). Using couple data as a methodological tool: The case of marital violence. *Journal of Marriage and the Family, 45,* 633–644.

Tyree, A., and Malone, J. (1991). *How can it be that wives hit husbands as much as husbands hit wives and none of us knew it?* Paper presented at the annual meeting of the American Sociological Association.

U.S. Department of Justice. (1976). *Dictionary of criminal justice data terminology*. Washington, DC: National Criminal Justice Information Service.

Vissing, Y. M., Straus, M. A., Gelles, R. J., and Harrop, J. W. (1991). Verbal aggression by parents and psychosocial problems of children. *Child Abuse and Neglect, 15*, 223–238.

Walker, L. E. A. (1984). *The battered woman syndrome*. New York: Springer.

Wolfgang, M. E. (1958). *Patterns of criminal homicide*. Philadelphia: University of Pennsylvania Press.

7

Domestic Violence Harms Both Men and Women

Tish Durkin

Tish Durkin is a contributing editor for Mademoiselle, *a monthly magazine for women.*

Stories about violent women—both fictitious and true—have been featured prominently in the media. Many have pointed to these stories as proof that women are as violent as men and that men suffer equally from domestic violence—arguments that have been used to discredit the legitimacy of women's claims of being battered by their male partners. Women are, in fact, victims of fatal and near-fatal violence more often than men. However, men are often victims of abuse, and their suffering should also be taken seriously.

A mousy housewife cuts off the penis of her sleeping husband, and the story makes headlines worldwide. Lorena Bobbitt of Manassas, Virginia, was acquitted of the charge of malicious wounding, but it is the act itself that no one can forget. No wonder men everywhere have been sitting with their knees together ever since.

Meanwhile, rumors flew about an alleged separation of Shannen Doherty and her husband, Ashley Hamilton, which they denied. With her history of being accused of assault, Doherty remains the national poster girl for female aggression: Men love her, leave her, and some take restraining orders out against her . . . or so we read in *People*.

Call it the year of the armed woman: In 1993, physically abusive female characters starred on television to great success. On one episode of the Emmy-award-winning series *Picket Fences*, a male calculus teacher was date-raped by a young woman wielding a hot iron. The CBS Tuesday Movie *Murder of Innocence* had a highly rated story line in which a wife guns down her husband. The huge audience response echoed similarly high sales of videos depicting violent women, from knife-wielding Glenn Close to ice pick–packing Sharon Stone.

What does it all mean?

Tish Durkin, "The Myth of the Violent Femme." This article first appeared in the April 1994 issue of *Mademoiselle* magazine and is reprinted by permission of the author.

Introducing . . . the Violent Femme

She can be either fictitious or flesh and blood; she can use her fists, a gun or knife to maim or kill a man in a love- or sex-related situation. One thing is certain: At a time when crime and violence are among the top concerns of Americans, the Violent Femme is a compelling vision—one of tabloid television's favorite subjects and a bottomless source of material for jokes and chatter among the general public. She has become a national figure.

But is she real? More importantly, is she on the rise—or even a trend? With all the media and mass cultural attention, we might easily believe that—having spent human history tied down, boxed in and beaten up—women are turning the tables of abuse on men. We might start to think that violence, like distance running, has become an American sport in which men are soon to be outdone. We might even conclude that the numbers of men suffering from battered-boyfriend syndrome will soon eclipse the amount of domestic violence cases perpetrated by men against women.

If so, we'd be dead wrong.

"These cases exist—I represented a guy battered by a wife who was on serious drugs," says Sheila James Kuehl, counsel to the California Women's Law Center. Yes, violent tendencies are by no means the province of men alone. But as Kuehl points out, all reliable statistics point in the other direction: When it comes to serious physical abuse, women are still overwhelmingly on the receiving end. Case studies indicate that while psychological profiles of battered men are similar to those of battered women, there are key differences that modify the nature and severity of abuse. And though abused men do not have the emergency support services available to their female counterparts, this may be precisely because they need them less.

So, while images of abusive women hog the spotlight, a disproportionate number of numbing stories about abused women are relegated to the back pages of newspapers—and the back burner of mass consciousness. Somewhere along the line, we've sharpened our appetites for these Violent Femme tales and lost our taste for the all-too-true stories of flesh-and-blood women who suffer at the hands of violent men.

Up in arms

First, a reality check: According to the National Crime Victimization Survey 1973–92, women are victims of family violence three times as often as men. Domestic violence affects a woman every 15 seconds and kills four women each day. Year after year, many more husbands and boyfriends kill wives and girlfriends than get killed by them.

That's not to say that women are all sweetness and light.

In 1975 and again in 1985, Murray Straus of the Family Research Institute at the University of New Hampshire conducted wide-ranging studies which found that wives assault their husbands as often as husbands assault their wives. In fact, Straus found, women were *more* likely than men to hit or threaten with a gun or knife, and as likely as men to use a weapon on their partner. Due to these findings, it became accurate to state that men fall victim to domestic violence as much as women do.

Angry men's magazines made new waves with these old numbers. *"We are the target,"* bellowed a headline in the August 1993 *Penthouse* (emphasis theirs). *"Men are at least as likely to suffer domestic violence as women,"* announced the text, taking Straus's message to the masses.

Given a closer look, the masses might not take this message too literally. Though Straus concludes that women are as likely to use a knife or gun against their partner, women don't seem to be shooting or stabbing as effectively as their mates: In 1992, when 383 wives killed their husbands, 913 husbands killed their wives. And since most men are bigger and stronger than most women, their fists, if so used, *are* weapons. Even if women strike men as often as men strike women, men hit harder. According to the U.S. Justice Department, women are the victims in roughly 95 percent of all types of domestic-violence cases. Allowing for conflicts between gay men, less than 5 percent of violence against another individual takes place at the hands of abusive women.

We might easily believe that—having spent human history tied down, boxed in and beaten up—women are turning the tables of abuse on men.

At the end of the *Penthouse* piece, an information box asked: "Have you been victimized?" followed by a 900 number. Months later, the magazine could identify no more than nine messages. Of course, this response occurred only within the scope of one magazine's circulation. According to the U.S. Justice Department, the number of reported cases of female violence in America amounts to fewer than 24,000 abused men. The 95 percent of cases in which women are assaulted by men adds up to—and this is a conservative estimate—*at least* 450,000 battered women.

It's not that many women don't hit men—Straus's study shows they do. But once the "violence equality" picture leaves the academic world or male-magazine pages, it looks different. Reality changes it. Even Straus himself agrees. "From a policy standpoint, the emphasis should be on battered women," he told the *New York Times* in 1992, "because women suffer by far the most injuries."

Suffering on both sides

Sad, but true: People of both genders do terrible things to the opposite sex. "I've interviewed men scalded by boiling water," says Dr. Malcolm George, a neurophysiologist at Queen Mary and Westfield College of the University of London and author of the study *Riding the Donkey Backwards: Men as the Unacceptable Victims of Marital Violence*. "One man's wife used to carry a hammer around in her handbag."

Such stories can ring a bell with anyone who knows a battered woman. "I have typed up temporary restraining orders for women who have had nails plunged up their vaginas," says Kathy Sallis, a legal advocate at Rainbow Services in San Pedro, California.

There are other areas, mostly psychological, where these stories are remarkably similar. The battered man endures the same torments—shock, rage, misplaced guilt—that the battered woman knows so well. He, like her, will agonize over whether to stay in the hostile situation or flee it. If he decides to stay, he often does for the same reason she does, be it worry about children or some form of dependence on his batterer. In short, abused men live much the same lives as abused women—until they start to deal with their problems. Then their paths diverge.

Men don't tell

For one thing, society discourages the male victim from coming forth. While in recent years a feminist climate has made it seem less difficult for women to speak up, men still have to deal with more ingrained sexual attitudes. "If a [battered] guy has the courage to dial 911," explains a male veteran who has been on both sides of domestic violence, "the cops see a guy and say, 'What's the matter, can't you handle the little woman?'"

The whole of Western culture stands behind that emasculating statement. While both men and women suffer shame in speaking up, victimized women aren't perceived as going against their gender identity. "Men are brought up to protect women, not to be beaten by them," points out Alvin Baraff, a clinical psychologist and founder of the Men-Center counseling service in Washington, D.C.

When a man does speak up—and thus becomes a male oddity—he faces the prospect of being either gossipworthy or newsworthy. Note how the life of Dean Factor, ex-friend of Violent Femme Shannen Doherty, became the subject of a media frenzy, and how journalists gave almost daily updates on the prognosis of John Bobbitt's member.

Currently, few services address a battered man's emotional—or even physical—problems. "Many battered men end up in homeless shelters, but otherwise there isn't the support for men that there is for women," says Dr. George. But, evidently, there is less of a need among male abuse victims for such services. The only battered men's shelter that existed in Great Britain, begun in November 1992, closed soon after it opened. None has replaced it.

When it comes to serious physical abuse, women are still overwhelmingly on the receiving end.

This may reflect battered men's reluctance to speak up, or society's reluctance to hear them. Yet it's hard to believe that there are enough physically endangered, socially silenced men out there to stack up against the numbers of abused women. Consider a single day's caseload at one Indianapolis battered women's shelter: Two fractured-rib cases, one woman with black eyes, one broken-nose case, one woman with both a broken leg and collarbone, a case in which the woman had bruises all over her body, two women with broken ankles—one of them with facial bruises as well. Add up the women across the country who take to shelters, emergency rooms and the streets because of intense and recurring physical violence, and you'll get a number close to 2.1 million women.

Of course, it shouldn't matter who gets hurt, as long as everybody who suffers gets help. Unfortunately, though, the amount of attention given to who gets hurt has a great deal to do with who gets helped. By focusing on the Violent Femme, and by implication the victimized male, our society threatens real women with real neglect. Because in order for budget dollars to keep flowing for female abuse victims, an awareness that there is a continual need for shelters must be maintained. "When men are battered at the same rate as women," says Carol Arthur, executive director of the Domestic Abuse Project in Minneapolis, Minnesota, "they can have an equal share of the [domestic-violence funding] money."

Men do leave

After victims admit the fact of abuse and utilize the support services that are available, they must decide whether or not to leave their abusive partners and their families. When domestic violence is a question of life or death, who survives depends upon who can get out. It is unfair to assume that men have fewer qualms than women about abandoning their families. But it's an airtight fact that they have more money. According to U.S. Census Bureau figures for 1992, about 42,245,000 husbands had jobs, earning a median income of $30,028. Only 33,990,000 wives—well more than 8 million fewer—worked outside the home, with a median income of $15,252 per year. So the typical American wife earns about half as much as her husband—if she earns anything at all. For the victim of domestic violence, the implication couldn't be clearer. "Men leave," says Kuehl of the California Women's Law Center, "and they *can* leave."

Just as money can free the battered man, the lack of it often traps the battered woman. Geneva Love, 29, is now serving a 17-years-to-life sentence in the Arkansas Women's Unit for the fatal shooting of her husband, Azell. Two days before the murder, when he finished beating her for the last of many times, all she asked him for was a bus ticket.

For women much more than men, the fact of fear is as cold as cash. There is no evidence that men's lives are commonly threatened by women they have left, but "seventy-five percent of the women killed by their mates are tracked down *after* they've left home," says Lee Rosen, chair of the American Bar Association's domestic-violence council and a divorce lawyer in Raleigh, North Carolina. "The most dangerous times of their lives is when they come to see me."

It became accurate to state that men fall victim to domestic violence as much as women do.

"Goodness and badness don't come from sex," asserts Dr. George. "We need to focus on real victims, irrespective of gender." It seems silly to fight over who suffers most.

But when faced with an onslaught of mythic Violent Femmes, real women must fight back. With the 15 to 20 years it took to establish the fact that domestic violence against women exists, we can't grow immune to hearing about it. Just because the Violent Femme pushes the boundaries of testosterone-driven imaginations—and feeds female revenge fantasies—that's no reason to let her camouflage the needs of female abuse victims. Or let men highlight instances of their own suffering as a form of backlash against the growing power of women.

This doesn't give us the right to dismiss men in pain. Certainly, women's increasingly accepted tendency to ridicule wounded men would be wildly put down if the genders were reversed. "I don't know of a single man," Baraff muses over some women's it's-about-time take on John Bobbitt's maiming, "who would express delight at hearing that another man had cut off a woman's breast."

A good point, but the same week that Lorena Bobbitt drew her world-famous knife, 24-year-old Elizabeth Lezuma of Kerrville, Texas, was stabbed in her right breast by her live-in lover.

Jacqueline Schultz, 30, of Rockford, Minnesota, was stabbed 14 times during an argument with her husband.

Elizabeth Delgado, 19, of Springfield, Massachusetts, was shot in a friend's car by her ex-boyfriend, who had just served 60 days in jail for violating an order to stay away from her.

They all died.

Did you read about that?

8

The Problem of Domestic Violence Is Exaggerated

Cathy Young

Cathy Young is the vice president of the Women's Freedom Network, a women's organization in Washington, D.C., that searches for approaches to many gender issues that are equally fair to both men and women.

With the charge that O.J. Simpson murdered his former wife, Nicole Brown, media attention on domestic violence increased dramatically. Unfortunately, the media and many advocates for battered women have grossly exaggerated the incidence and seriousness of the problem for women. The exaggeration undermines public sympathy and support for both male and female victims of domestic violence.

It did not take long for advocacy groups and some commentators to claim that the O.J. Simpson case could do for domestic violence what Anita Hill did for sexual harassment. If the Anita Hill analogy refers to gender politics eclipsing truth, common sense, and journalistic skepticism, then that is exactly what's happening.

We are barraged with horrendous figures. CNN's Sheryl Potts said at the end of a 3.5-minute segment on wife-abuse, "While you were watching this, 13 women were severely beaten by someone who claims to love them" (i.e., one every 15 seconds). According to the Associated Press, "4 million to 6 million women are beaten [each year]. That means once every 5 seconds . . . a woman is punched or kicked . . . or held down and pummeled." On *Crossfire*, Miami radio talk-show host Pat Stevens upped the count to 60 million by reasoning that "there are 6 million reported cases," and "the FBI estimates" that only 1 in 10 is reported. This went unchallenged.

One AP report ran somewhat counter to the general tone, noting that murders of women by male partners had dropped 18 per cent since the late 1970s; but it went on to temper this unduly optimistic message with the assertion that non-fatal violence was up: "From 1980 to 1990, federal

Cathy Young, "Abused Statistics," *National Review*, August 1, 1994; ©1994 by National Review, Inc., 150 E. 35th St., New York, NY 10016. Reprinted by permission.

figures show, reports of domestic assault . . . rose from 2 million to 4 million, according to Rita Smith, coordinator for the National Coalition Against Domestic Violence."

Where do the numbers come from? One source for the 4-to-6-million figure is a 1993 Commonwealth Fund study, which included such acts as shoving, slapping, and throwing things in its definition of battering. The statistic of a woman beaten every 15 seconds is derived from the 1985 National Family Violence Survey by University of New Hampshire researchers Murray Straus and Richard Gelles, which estimated that about 1.8 million American women each year suffer at least one incident of "severe violence" by a partner—a punch, a kick, an assault with an object. But only 7 per cent of the victims required medical care. A study published in *Archives of Internal Medicine* in 1992 found that, based on reports by wives in marital therapy, 48 per cent of "severe marital aggression" by husbands caused no injury, and 31 per cent caused only a "superficial bruise." While these are still reprehensible acts, most people visualize something very different when they think of "severe violence."

And the reports of domestic assault rising from 2 to 4 million a year over a decade? The figure, said Rita Smith, came from the Justice Department's Bureau of Justice Statistics. Were these assaults reported to police? "Either that, or to medical personnel," said Miss Smith. "I'm not exactly sure how they gathered it, but it was one of the statistics they put out in some publication." What publication? She didn't recall.

An information specialist at the BJS knew nothing of such figures. Most of the Bureau's publications are based on the National Crime Victimization Survey, which puts the number of female victims of assaults by partners at about 470,000 a year.

In 33 domestic murders, 32 couples had no prior police record of battery.

Another shocking claim was made in a *MacNeil/Lehrer NewsHour* segment by Connie McCall of Rainbow Services, a battered-women's assistance group in Los Angeles: "Over 50 per cent of women admitted to emergency rooms are admitted for an injury caused by a partner." In a pre–O.J. Simpson speech in March 1994, Health and Human Services Secretary Donna Shalala gave a more modest estimate: "In our hospital emergency rooms, some 20 to 30 per cent of women arrive because of physical abuse by their partner."

These numbers (whose implausibility ought to be evident to anyone who has ever been to a hospital) come in part from studies in which medical charts were reviewed and most unexplained or inadequately explained injuries to women were reclassified as related to abuse, and in part from a 1984 study based on questionnaires distributed to emergency-room patients in a Detroit hospital. About 25 per cent of the female patients answered "yes" to the statement, "At some time my boyfriend/husband or girlfriend/wife has pushed me around, hit me, kicked me, or hurt me"; so did about 20 per cent of the men. Most of the abuse did not seem to be directly related to the emergency-room visit. Moreover, a high percentage of the subjects were poor, unemployed, and cohabiting without marriage—factors strongly associated with the risk of domestic violence.

The same fallacy of projecting data obtained by studying the urban poor to the population at large is responsible for another widely reported figure—cited, for instance, in *Newsweek*'s July 4, 1994, cover story on battered women: "[I]n 1992 the U.S. Surgeon General ranked abuse by husbands and partners as the leading cause of injuries to women aged 15 to 44." In fact, in a 1992 column in the *Journal of the American Medical Association* on the medical response to domestic abuse, then-Surgeon General Antonia Novello mentioned that "One study found violence to be . . . the leading cause of injuries to women ages 15 through 44." This refers to *all* violence, not just violence by male partners. The article in which the finding was reported, titled "A Population-Based Study of Injuries in Inner City Women," examines emergency-room visits by women "in a poor, urban, black community in western Philadelphia."

And how many women are killed by their current or former mates? CNN has cited the figure of 4,000 a year—even though the FBI statistic is 1,300 to 1,400. The higher number comes from activist groups and includes, Miss Smith told me, "a lot of suspicious deaths that aren't [officially] classified as a homicide." The higher the better: on *This Week with David Brinkley*, Lynne Gold-Bikin, incoming chairman of the American Bar Association's family-law section, claimed that "some 25 per cent of women who are abused ultimately get killed by their husbands." If, as *Newsweek* says, "1 woman in 4 will be physically assaulted in her lifetime," this would put a woman's risk of being murdered by a partner at 1 in 16. In fact, it's closer to 1 in 1,000.

A widely cited statistic—which appeared in Sheryl Potts's CNN report—is that "women who leave their batterers are at a 75 per cent greater risk of being killed by the batterer than those who stay." This information was attributed to the NCADV; a brochure issued by the organization cites "Barbara Hart, 1988," as the source. When I asked Miss Smith about this, she said a bit hesitantly, "Barbara Hart is an attorney with the Pennsylvania Coalition Against Domestic Violence—and I have recently talked to her and she said, 'I didn't say that.' So, the figure—whether or not it's 75 per cent, I don't know. [But] most of the women who are murdered are either separated or in the process of leaving when they die." She assumed that all these women had been battered in the marriage. However, a number of experts such as criminologist Lawrence Sherman, president of the Crime Control Institute and author of *Policing Domestic Violence* (1992), dispute the "escalation" theory. Sherman's study in Milwaukee over nearly two years revealed that in 33 domestic murders, 32 couples had no prior police record of battery—and there was 1 homicide among the roughly 6,500 couples with such records.

Epidemic proportions?

Is there an epidemic of domestic violence in America? One could say that we have an epidemic of violence in general, and for all the talk about doctors and executives who beat their wives, domestic violence tends to affect primarily the same segments of society as street crime. Men and, to a lesser extent, women guilty of violence in the home are also much more likely than other people to commit violent acts outside the family. Yet the view that domestic violence is largely the doing of a minority of thugs and sociopaths is anathema to the highly politicized battered-women's advocacy movement. An NCADV pamphlet makes this clear: "A feminist-based analysis of battering [shifts] from a focus on the 'pathology' of individuals or families to the particular social policies, norms, and practices which tolerate woman-abuse."

The theme of supposed tolerance for woman-battering in our culture is reflected in the infamous tale of the "rule of thumb," repeated by Cokie Roberts on *This Week with David Brinkley:* "The rule of thumb, the expression we use . . . that was the size of the stick that was acceptable to beat your wife with under common law." Yet, as the scholar Christina Hoff Sommers shows in *Who Stole Feminism?* this origin of the phrase "rule of thumb" is a myth. While two American courts in the nineteenth century alluded to such an "ancient law" they never invoked it as a standard. The first legal code enacted by the Massachusetts colonists in 1652 *prohibited* wife-beating.

Despite attempts to find the roots of wife-battering in the power of physical chastisement once given to husbands by law, few serious researchers believe that domestic violence is primarily a way to maintain patriarchal control. Even feminist scholar Elizabeth Schneider of Brooklyn Law School concedes, in a 1992 *New York University Law Review* article, that the "traditional model" of battering as a means of maintaining male dominance "is thrown into question when the violent partner is a woman, or the victim is a man." Though Professor Schneider is referring to same-sex couples, a wealth of research (notably the Straus-Gelles studies) has found that wives and girlfriends are the aggressors at least half the time, though they are five to six times less likely to cause physical damage. (On one *MacNeil/Lehrer* report, an L.A. police officer said that he had been on many calls where the woman was the assailant; but the panel discussion following the segment focused solely on male batterers and female victims.)

Male violence toward women fits into the fashionable larger theme of oppression; female violence toward men does not.

For every two women killed by a male partner, there is at least one man killed by a wife or girlfriend—not including cases dismissed as self-defense. It is interesting to recall that in 1989, when San Diego housewife Betty Broderick fatally shot her ex-husband and his new wife after harassing them for months, the incident was not seen as emblematic of the epidemic of domestic violence by women. Indeed, Mrs. Broderick got a great deal of sympathy as a wronged wife (she claimed that Dan Broderick's alimony payments of only $16,000 *a month* amounted to a white-collar version of battery), and her first trial ended with a hung jury. Male violence toward women fits into the fashionable larger theme of oppression; female violence toward men does not.

With remarkable lack of compunction about exploiting a horrible tragedy for political gain, members of the National Organization for Women, with Patricia Schroeder and other congresswomen on hand, rallied on Capitol Hill to urge passage of the Violence Against Women Act—which, among other things, would redefine wife-beating as a gender-based hate crime and mandate sensitivity training for judges. (In Massachusetts, a similar media frenzy has already led to a situation in which, former Massachusetts Bar Association President Elaine Epstein wrote in 1993, "it has become essentially impossible to effectively represent a man against whom any allegation of domestic violence has been made.")

Beyond these immediate political goals, the advocates' real agenda is to promote their view that American women are routinely terrorized by men who are intent on keeping them subjugated. Why not just say that 5 out of 4 women are battered by men, and be done with it? Given their track records, the media would probably buy that one, too.

9

Women Are Responsible for Domestic Violence

Katherine Dunn

Katherine Dunn is the author of the novel Geek Love, *a reporter, and a contributor to such journals as the* New Republic, Mother Jones, *and* Esquire.

Media coverage of the O.J. Simpson murder case has helped perpetuate the violent man–nonviolent woman stereotype. It is time to realize that women initiate and engage in physical violence against their male partners as often as men do so against women. Presenting a stereotype as the truth does little to solve the problem of domestic violence for either men or women.

An irritating by-product of the O.J. Simpson tragedy is the blizzard of balderdash about wife battering that has been loosed in the mainstream media. [O.J. Simpson's ex-wife, Nicole Brown, was murdered on June 12, 1994. Simpson was later arrested and tried for the murder.] The double murders and the melodramatic events surrounding them are the latest pretext for spreading the anti-male propaganda that passes as socially responsible concern over domestic violence. Men are violent and therefore bad. Women are nonviolent and therefore good.

Let us note that on February 22, Maria Montalvo, a registered nurse in New Jersey, punished her husband for moving out after she had assaulted him. She drove their two preschool children to her husband's parents' house, where he was staying, and parked the car out front. She then doused the toddlers with gasoline and set them on fire. The burning car ignited another vehicle nearby and prevented the grandparents from rescuing them. Montalvo, whose husband had previously filed several complaints of assault to the police, is awaiting trial. Yet this case did not trigger a national discussion of how dangerous it is to leave a battering spouse. No domestic violence workers came forward in 1992 to decry the typical pattern of stalking, harassing phone calls and destruction of property that San Diego socialite Betty Broderick inflicted on her ex-husband before she murdered him and his new wife in their bed.

Katherine Dunn, "Truth Abuse," *The New Republic*, August 1, 1994. Reprinted by permission of *The New Republic*; ©1994 The New Republic, Inc.

We are not being told the truth about domestic violence. For starters, it is nowhere near as extensive as the media is claiming. Stories published since the Simpson murders claim that 2 million to 4 million women are beaten by their male partners regularly. Terms such as "epidemic" are tossed around, along with estimates that violence plagues 50 percent or more of all relationships. Yet two of the most respected researchers in the field of domestic violence, sociologists Murray Straus of the University of New Hampshire and Richard Gelles of the University of Rhode Island, found in their 1985 National Family Violence Survey that 84 percent of American families are not violent. Among the 16 percent that are, only 3 to 4 percent include family members who engage in extreme violence (such as punching, kicking, using weapons).

Women abuse men, too

Some advocacy groups claim that 4,000 women are killed by spousal abuse every year. But in 1992, in the high-risk group of women aged 18 to 34, there was a sufficiently grisly total of 702 fatalities. A Justice Department study, released July 10, 1994, reveals that among white spousal murder victims, 38 percent were male and 62 percent were female. Among black couples, 47 percent were male and 53 percent were female. A new study of FBI and census data by James Alan Fox, dean of Northeastern University's College of Criminal Justice, shows a drop of 18 percent in the overall rate of women killed by husbands or boyfriends since the late 1970s. And, though a majority of child sexual molestation is committed by men, the Justice Department found that women are responsible for more than half of the cases of child murder.

An irritating by-product of the O.J. Simpson tragedy is the blizzard of balderdash about wife battering that has been loosed in the mainstream media.

Straus and Gelles are two of the many researchers who have found domestic violence distributed equally between the sexes. In anonymous interviews with families randomly picked from the general population for their surveys, they found that half of all domestic violence involved mutual battery—both spouses brawling. In about half the cases of mutual battering, women were the instigators—the ones who slapped, slugged or swung weapons first. Male violence against passive wives occurred in one-quarter of the incidents; in another quarter of the incidents, women were the violent partners who attacked nonviolent spouses. When only the women's version of events was reported, the results were the same. And men were still equally victimized when only the most severe forms of violence were analyzed. "The main conclusion to be drawn from these findings," wrote the researchers, "is that women not only engage in physical violence as often as men, but they also initiate violence as often as men."

Advocacy groups often cite studies that show that 94 percent of battered women never hit back, but these are from very limited, self-selected groups who are actually in shelters or filing police reports. An accurate measure of the violence in the general population can only be made through large-scale, scientifically random surveys such as those conducted by Straus and Gelles.

Considering the hysterical tone of the hype, it's ironic that the actual rate of violence against women has dropped steadily since 1975 but the rate of female violence against men has stayed the same. "Violence by wives has not been an object of public concern," Gelles and Straus note. "There has been no publicity, and no funds have been invested in ameliorating this problem because it has not been defined as a problem."

We are not being told the truth about domestic violence.

One group that takes female violence seriously is the lesbian community, in which battery is a profoundly disturbing concern that is rarely discussed publicly. Martin Hiraga, director of the Anti-Violence Project for the National Gay and Lesbian Task Force, says that although no national studies have yet been done, all the available evidence points to domestic violence in lesbian couples occurring "no more and no less often than in heterosexual couples."

But this is not the picture of domestic violence that most of us see. Instead, we are presented with the image of males as the perpetrators of all violence toward women and children, and women as blameless, powerless, always nurturing victims. In cases where a wife attacks her husband, we are told, it is always an act of self-defense, brought on by years of escalating abuse. Men who are abused by their wives are fodder for jokes. Women who are abused by their husbands can get away with murder.

The last national misinformation campaign about domestic violence was the great Super Bowl hoax of 1993. Advocacy groups claimed that watching football triggered male violence and that Super Bowl Sunday was the worst day of the year for wife-beating in the United States. That fiction was exposed, but the alleged football connection to domestic violence has been revived, with former all-star running back O.J. Simpson offered as proof that competitive sports inflame male brutality. No responsible editor would tolerate claims that the Simpson case proved that all black people are violent or that mixed marriages don't work. But the assumption that Simpson beat his wife because he is male and an athlete is accepted without question.

To complicate matters, radical women's groups actively oppose the spreading of more accurate information about gender equity in family violence. Take the case of Dr. Suzanne Steinmetz, director of the Family Research Institute at Indiana University-Purdue University at Indianapolis. When her article, "The Battered Husband Syndrome," appeared in the journal *Victimology* in 1978, she was harassed by phone, there were threats to harm her children, her colleagues were lobbied to prevent her getting tenure and bomb threats were sent to a branch of the American Civil Liberties Union that had invited her to give a talk. Other researchers in the field report similar experiences, and male researchers are commonly accused of being batterers themselves.

These misconceptions not only hurt men; they also hurt women by inaccurately portraying them as weak children who cannot stand up for themselves but must be defended at all times. As Rene Denfeld, author of *The New Victorians*, points out, "Protectionism is the key to sexism." The denial of female aggression is a destructive social myth. It robs an entire gender of a significant spectrum of power, leaving women less than equal with men and effectively keeping them "in their place" and under control. It is understandable that those who work with victims of violence should be extreme in defense of victims' rights, but deliberately ignoring a full 50 percent of the domestic violence problem guarantees that it will not be solved.

In the long term, appealing to women's physical weakness is a lousy strategy for feminists. As we claim our ability and our right to be fire fighters, police officers, jet pilots, surgeons or basketball stars, we must also own up to our uglier capacities. Those include the potential to batter our partners.

10

The Media Misreport Domestic Violence

John Leo

John Leo is an editorialist for U.S. News & World Report, *a weekly newsmagazine.*

Statistics reported by the media are inflated and skewed in an attempt to portray domestic violence as a gender war in which brutish males are oppressing innocent, passive females. In fact, men and women abuse their partners at equal rates.

Journalists are having a lot of trouble dealing with the issue of domestic violence. No other current topic seems so steeped in myths, bad stats and general misinformation.

Take "the rule of thumb," for example, tossed into the discussion this time around by the *Los Angeles Times* and the Brinkley show, among others. It's supposed to be a rule in English common law that men are allowed to beat their wives with a stick no thicker than one's thumb. But it's not in the common law, as Christina Hoff Sommers shows in her book *Who Stole Feminism?* It's a fable, designed to make the legal system look like an instrument males use against women.

Or take the well-traveled factoid that "At least one fifth of all emergency room visits by women are the result of beating by men" (*New York Newsday*). That finding comes from an inner-city population in Detroit. It can't be projected nationwide. And besides, that Detroit statistic on beaten people includes men hit by women.

Crazy stats are hurled around creatively without challenge. Pat Stevens, a talk-show host, said on *Crossfire,* "There are 6 million women a year in this country who are battered by their husbands or boyfriends." That's true if you extend the definition of battering far enough. One push, shove or slap on the arm a year will get you listed among the 6 million spouse-batterers, just like O.J. Simpson. If you clutch your spouse's elbow as she walks away from an argument, that counts too.

On the assumption that only 10 percent of batterings are reported, Stevens told Michael Kinsley and John Sununu that an estimated 60 mil-

John Leo, "Is It a War Against Women?" *U.S. News & World Report*, July 11, 1994; ©1994, U.S. News & World Report. Reprinted with permission.

lion American women are beaten each year by husbands or boyfriends. What Kinsley or Sununu might have said, but didn't, is that 60 million would be a very surprising total, since the Census Bureau estimates that only 56.8 million women in America are living with a man.

Hard facts

The real numbers are shocking enough. About 1.8 million women suffer real violence from husbands or boyfriends, meaning one or more incidents of hitting or kicking each year, with about 10 percent requiring help from a doctor, according to Murray Straus of the University of New Hampshire, an important researcher in the field, and co-author of *Intimate Violence* with researcher Richard Gelles. This means about 3 percent of women living with men suffer at least one violent act a year, with about one third of 1 percent requiring medical help.

Many studies show that the real numbers are low. In 1993, a Commonwealth Fund survey asked 2,500 women about domestic incidents in the previous 12 months. Here are some questions, with the percentage that said yes: Did your spouse or partner ever throw something at you? (3 percent), push, grab, shove or slap? (5 percent), kick, bite, hit with a fist or an object? (2 percent), beat you up or choke you? (zero percent), use or threaten to use a knife or a gun? (zero percent).

Numbers fed to the media are not just routinely exaggerated and massaged into an "epidemic" of violence; they are presented as somehow very different from the rest of the violence in a violent society: They are offered up as evidence of a gender war that implicates men in general, and the whole society, in the battering conducted by out-of-control males.

Domestic violence can be portrayed as a war against women, but only if a lot of evidence is suppressed or explained away.

These days, it's fairly routine to see journalism endorsing the radical theory of domestic violence as gender warfare. Domestic violence can be portrayed as a war against women, but only if a lot of evidence is suppressed or explained away.

Factors such as this, for instance:

• A Straus and Gelles study showed that 1.8 million women reported assaults from their men and 2 million men reported assaults from their women.

• The 1985 National Family Violence Survey showed that men and women were abusing one another in roughly equal numbers. (Men typically do far more damage, but the number of attacks is the same.)

• Male gays and lesbians report rates of domestic violence and abuse at least as high as those among heterosexuals. One study shows an abuse rate of 14 percent among male gays and 46 percent among lesbians in their current relationships. Is this gender warfare too?

• Contrary to claims that women's domestic violence is largely a defensive reaction to male violence, a 1993 study by Straus and Gelles found, Straus says, that "women initiate assaults against their partners at the same rate as men. It isn't just self-defense, as I claimed in my 1988 book." Why did he claim that in the book? "It was the politically correct position." Other studies back him up. One in 1990 concluded that 24 percent of domestic violence is initiated by women, 27 percent by men.

The radical view of domestic violence (it's the patriarchy in action, oppressing women) simply doesn't fit the accumulating evidence. It's a highly ideological overlay, dividing the world unrealistically into brutish males and innocent, passive females. How long will this wrongheaded oppressor-victim framework dominate press coverage of the issue?

11

Men and Women Both Cause Domestic Violence

Judith Sherven and James Sniechowski

Judith Sherven is a clinical psychologist. James Sniechowski holds a Ph.D. in human behavior. Together they are consultants who work with corporations on gender issues.

Society clings to the image of women as sweet and innocent, but women are in fact equal participants in domestic violence. The solution to the problem will not be found until women and society in general acknowledge that domestic violence is the responsibility of both men and women.

Once again, the myth of the evil, brutal male perpetrator and the perfect, innocent female victim is being broadcast and written about as gospel. The discussion is national. The rage and sorrow, palpable. Only when we come to terms with the fact that domestic violence is the responsibility of both men and women, however, can we put a stop to this horrible nightmare.

Domestic violence is not an either-or phenomenon. It is not either the man's fault or the woman's. It is a both-and problem. Both the male and the female are bound in their dance of mutual destructiveness, their incapacity for intimacy and appreciation of differences. They need each other to perpetuate personal and collective dramas of victimization and lovelessness, and so, regrettably, neither can leave.

A new perspective

This is a very untidy idea for people who have grown up with movies in which the "good guy" triumphs over the "bad guy" and rescues the damsel from distress. But to tackle the plague of domestic violence, we must alter our perspective. Facts:

• Forty-one percent of spousal murders are committed by wives, according to a special report entitled, "Murder in Families," issued by the U.S. Department of Justice, Bureau of Justice Statistics in July 1994.

Judith Sherven and James Sniechowski, "Women Are Responsible, Too," *Los Angeles Times*, June 21, 1994. Reprinted by permission.

• The 1985 National Family Violence Survey, funded by the National Institute of Mental Health and supported by many other surveys, revealed that women and men were physically abusing one another in roughly equal numbers. Wives reported that they were more often the aggressors. Using weapons to make up for physical disadvantage, they were not just fighting back.

• While 1.8 million women annually suffered one or more assaults from a husband or boyfriend, 2 million men were assaulted by a wife or girlfriend, according to a 1986 study on U.S. family violence published in the *Journal of Marriage and Family*. That study also found that 54% of all violence termed "severe" was by women.

• The *Journal for the National Assn. of Social Workers* found in 1986 that among teen-agers who date, girls were violent more frequently than boys.

• Mothers abuse their children at a rate approaching twice that of fathers, according to state child-protective service agencies surveyed by the Children's Rights Coalition.

• Because men have been taught to "take it like a man" and are ridiculed when they reveal they have been battered by women, women are nine times more likely to report their abusers to the authorities.

Women are part and parcel of domestic violence.

In 1988, R.L. McNeeley, a professor at the School of Social Welfare of the University of Wisconsin, published "The Truth About Domestic Violence: A Falsely Framed Issue" [in *Social Work*], again revealing the level of violence against men by women. Such facts, though, are "politically incorrect." Even 10 years earlier, Susan Steinmetz, director of the Family Research Institute at Indiana University–Purdue University, received threats of harm to her children from radical women's groups after she published "The Battered Husband Syndrome" [in *Victimology*].

Why are we so surprised and appalled that men hit and abuse women who are physically smaller when women regularly hit and abuse small children?

Why are we, as a culture, loath to expose the responsibility of women in domestic abuse? Why do we cling to the pure and virginal image of the "sweet young thing" and the "damsel in distress"? If we are sincere about change, we must acknowledge the truth: Women are part and parcel of domestic violence.

Why does our culture refuse to hold women as well as men accountable for their participation in domestic violence? All of such women's behavior, whether perpetrator or victim, is understood and passed off as the by-product of socialization or poor economic status. On the other hand, men are held fully accountable for all of their behavior—despite the tough-guy stereotype all boys are encouraged to embody and the abuse many bear as a "normal and loving" part of their upbringing.

Some will argue that women fall into "spousal abuse syndrome," in which female passivity is explained as the result of the male brainwashing the female into believing that she is the cause of his violence. Consequently, she is powerless to alter the situation. But the truth is that all females receive some form of the following lessons: "You must cater to a man's ego," "You're nothing without a man" and "It's just as easy to love a rich man."

Girls often acquire this garbage from insecure mothers who believe that they are doing what is best for their daughters. If women are not expected to think and act for themselves, if their self-esteem is in shambles and their dependency is characterized as "feminine," the fault cannot be laid at the feet of men.

None of this is intended to exonerate O.J. Simpson [who was arrested and tried for the June 1994 murder of his ex-wife Nicole Simpson]. If he is guilty of the murders with which he has been charged, he must answer for his actions. The point is that, in the reaction to this sensational case, we do ourselves a grave disservice to slip into a gender-biased frenzy, vilifying and accusing only men as abusers.

The women's movement claims its goal to be equal rights for women. If that is so, then women must share responsibility for their behavior and their contribution to domestic violence. Otherwise, we remain in a distortion that overshadows the truth. Only the truth will show us the way out of the epidemic of violence that is destroying our families and our nation.

12

The Problem of
Domestic Violence
for Men Is Exaggerated

Ellis Cose

Ellis Cose is a contributing editor for Newsweek, *a weekly news-magazine.*

Many of those discussing the problem of domestic violence cite statistics purporting to show that women abuse men as often as men abuse women. Yet the same statistics, carefully examined, also show that women are injured more seriously and more often than men. Exaggerating the seriousness of domestic violence against men will prevent the public from taking a legitimate problem seriously.

Though the O.J. Simpson case put marital violence on virtually every editor's agenda, the leaders of what is sometimes called the men's movement are not particularly happy with the result. Coverage has focused too much, they say, on evil male perpetrators and innocent female victims. To read the papers, Nicole Simpson is Everywoman, and O.J. Simpson is Everyman. So, taking a cue from women's rights groups, the men's advocates have taken the offensive, putting forth statistics and anecdotes to argue that for every victimized female there exists a suffering, battered male.

Mel Feit, director of the National Center for Men, contends that men have been too silent for too long. He believes battered men are treated with no more respect (by either the press or the public) than abused women were 15 or 20 years ago. One-sided coverage, he argues, only aggravates the problem it supposedly aspires to illuminate.

Bogus information

Yet in their rush to correct the record, some of these spokesmen go overboard, presenting information that is frankly bogus. Many advocates insist, for instance, that women are as murderous as men—"half of spousal murders are committed by wives, a statistic that has been stable over time," declared a recent op-ed article in the *Los Angeles Times*. In fact, according to FBI statistics, the odds are nearly 2.4 times more likely that a husband will kill his wife than that she will kill him. In 1992, 1,432 women were killed by their "intimate" male partners; 623 men were killed by their female partners.

Men's activists are on firmer ground when they point to a 1985 study, funded by the National Institute of Mental Health, that found women to be as physically abusive as men. But even those results must be interpreted with care. That finding applies primarily, said one NIMH psychologist, to "moderate aggression" such as pushing and shoving. The "severe" aggression likely to land someone in a hospital is much more characteristic of men.

This does not mean that women are angels. David Gremillion, a University of North Carolina physician with a practice in Raleigh, North Carolina, says in most cases he sees "both partners are violent." In some instances (particularly involving elderly patients, or young men weakened by the AIDS virus), the female caretaker is the batterer. A new analysis by the Bureau of Justice Statistics found that, among blacks, wives and husbands did indeed kill each other at roughly equal rates. It also found that women were more prone than men to kill their offspring, and significantly more inclined to kill sons than daughters.

According to FBI statistics, the odds are nearly 2.4 times more likely that a husband will kill his wife than that she will kill him.

Nonetheless, the image of hordes of women wielding guns, knives, broomsticks or brass knuckles to terrorize their husbands is likely a fantasy. Certainly, some women resemble that description. Patricia Overberg, director of the Antelope Valley Domestic Violence Council in Lancaster, California, has counseled a few of them. And she runs the only shelter in America, she believes, that accepts abused men and women alike. Only five men have stayed there in the past three years. Fear of ridicule, she suspects, has kept the numbers down.

George Gilliland is one man who refuses to be cowed by the prospect of mockery. In December 1993, in a three-story building in St. Paul, Minnesota, he opened the only battered men's shelter in the country. By his count, 54 men have already used the facility. It is worth noting, however, that Gilliland is not your typical saint. He's had his own domestic troubles: judges have issued orders of protection against him. A grown son told the *St. Paul Pioneer Press* that Gilliland beat him as a child. And he was convicted of disorderly conduct on the complaint of two female domestic-abuse workers who claim he threatened them.

Gilliland sees conspiracy in the criticisms. The current raft of charges, he says, come from enemies out to discredit him, an unethical press and a vengeful son. As for the orders of protection, he scoffs, "The last I knew I had about 13 of these things [filed against him]. . . . What the media doesn't say, though . . . is that I turned around and also filed for orders of protection. And those were also put into effect against the same people that applied for them against me."

Despite the controversy swirling around him, Gilliland does seem to have done some good. "Pascal" (who asked not to be identified) lived in the shelter for several weeks in 1994. He was desperate to escape a cocaine-abusing girlfriend who pummelled him without provocation, he said. He was grateful that Gilliland provided a sanctuary for him and his 3-year-old daughter. "It gave me a chance to ease my mind," he says.

Men's groups are on to something important when they argue for a broader dialogue on domestic abuse. As Judith Sherven, a psychologist in Los Angeles, observed, "We're talking about . . . dynamics that both people bring to the experience that results in violence." In such cases, simply branding the man a batterer solves nothing. The couple (or perhaps the entire family) needs help to climb out of a morass of mutually reinforcing pathologies. A dialogue that distorts the facts, on either side, however, is not likely to provide them with that help.

Organizations to Contact

The editors have compiled the following list of organizations concerned with the issues debated in this book. The descriptions are derived from materials provided by the organizations. All have publications or information available for interested readers. The list was compiled on the date of publication of the present volume; names, addresses, and phone numbers may change. Be aware that many organizations take several weeks or longer to respond to inquiries, so allow as much time as possible.

Center for the Prevention of Sexual and Domestic Violence (CPSDV)
936 N. 34th St., Suite 200
Seattle, WA 98013
(206) 634-1903
fax: (206) 634-0115

CPSDV is an educational resource center that works with both religious and secular communities throughout the United States and Canada to address issues of sexual abuse and domestic violence. The center offers workshops concerning clergy misconduct, spouse abuse, child sexual abuse, rape, and pornography. Materials available from CPSDV include the quarterly journal *Working Together*, the book *Violence in the Family—a Workshop Curriculum for Clergy and Other Helpers*, the booklet *Keeping the Faith: Questions and Answers for the Abused Woman*, and the monograph *The Speaking Profits Us: Violence in the Lives of Women of Color*.

Center for Women Policy Studies (CWPS)
2000 P St. NW, Suite 508
Washington, DC 20036
(202) 872-1770

CWPS is a feminist policy research and advocacy organization that sponsors numerous programs dealing with women's issues, including educational equity, violence against women, and women's health programs. The center's publications on domestic violence include the policy paper *Violence Against Women as Bias-Motivated Hate Crime: Defining the Issues*, the handbook *Legal Help for Battered Women*, and fact sheets on girls and violence and violence against women.

Emerge: Counseling and Education to Stop Male Violence
2380 Massachusetts Ave., Suite 101
Cambridge, MA 02140
(617) 422-1550

Emerge works to prevent domestic violence by providing counseling services and training workshops for batterers. It also conducts research and disseminates information and referrals. Publications available from Emerge include an annual newsletter and the articles "Counseling Men Who Batter: A Pro-Feminist Analysis of Treatment Models" and "The Addicted or Alcoholic Batterer."

89

Family Research Laboratory (FRL)
University of New Hampshire
126 Horton Social Science Center
Durham, NH 03824-3586
(603) 862-1888
fax: (603) 862-1122

Since 1975, FRL has devoted itself primarily to understanding the causes and consequences of family violence, and it works to dispel myths about family violence through public education. It publishes numerous books and articles on violence between men and women, the physical abuse of spouses or co-habitants, marital rape, and verbal aggression. Books available from FRL include *When Battered Women Kill* and *Physical Violence in American Families: Risk Factors and Adaptations to Violence in 8,145 Families.*

Family Violence Prevention Fund (FVPF)
383 Rhode Island St., Suite 304
San Francisco, CA 94103
(415) 252-8900
fax: (415) 252-8991

FVPF is a national nonprofit organization concerned with domestic violence education, prevention, and public policy reform. It works to improve health care for battered women and to strengthen the judicial system's capacity to respond appropriately to domestic violence cases. The fund publishes brochures, action kits, and general information packets on domestic violence as well as the books *Domestic Violence: The Law and Criminal Prosecution, Domestic Violence: The Crucial Role of the Judge in Criminal Court Cases—a National Model for Judicial Education,* and *Domestic Violence in Immigrant and Refugee Communities: Asserting the Rights of Battered Women.*

Movement for the Establishment of Real Gender Equality (MERGE)
10011 116 St., #501
Edmonton, AB T5K 1V4
CANADA
(403) 488-4593

MERGE works to end gender discrimination and stereotyping. It contends that publicity about family violence is biased toward women and ignores the male victims of spousal abuse. MERGE disseminates educational information on gender issues, including the pamphlet *Balancing the Approach to Spouse Abuse.*

National Center on Women and Family Law (NCWFL)
799 Broadway, Suite 402
New York, NY 10003
(212) 674-8200

The center monitors and analyzes legal developments pertaining to domestic violence and family law issues, particularly those that affect low-income women and families. NCWFL operates the National Battered Women's Law Project and conducts research on domestic violence. It produces numerous publications, including research findings and a national newsletter for advocates of victims of domestic violence.

National Coalition Against Domestic Violence (NCADV)
PO Box 18749
Denver, CO 80218-0749
(303) 839-1852

NCADV is a nonprofit organization that helps empower battered women. It serves as a national information and referral network on domestic violence issues. Its publications include the position paper *A Current Analysis of the Battered Women's Movement*, the *National Directory of Domestic Violence Programs: A Guide to Community Shelter, Safe Home, and Service Programs*, the quarterly newsletter *NCADV Update*, and fact sheets on domestic violence, children and violence, and lesbian battering.

National Resource Center on Domestic Violence (NRC)
6400 Flank Dr., Suite 1300
Harrisburg, PA 17112-2778
(800) 537-2238
fax: (717) 545-9456

Established by the Pennsylvania Coalition Against Domestic Violence, NRC focuses on civil and criminal justice issues, child protection and custody issues, and health care access for battered women and their children. The center works to expand the service capacity of community-based domestic violence programs and state coalitions and assists government agencies, policy leaders, and other supporters of victims of domestic violence. NRC publications include brochures, videos, and posters on domestic violence as well as the manuals *Confronting Domestic Violence: Effective Police Response, Battering and Addiction*, and *Accountability: Program Standards for Battered Intervention Services*.

National Victims Resource Center (NVRC)
Box 6000
Rockville, MD 20850
(800) 627-6872

Established in 1983 by the U.S. Department of Justice's Office for Victims of Crime, NVRC is the primary source of information for crime victims. It answers questions by using national and regional statistics, a comprehensive collection of research findings, and a well-established network of victim advocates and organizations. NVRC distributes all Office of Justice Programs publications on victim-related issues, including a resource packet dedicated to domestic violence issues.

Women's Freedom Network (WFN)
4410 Massachusetts Ave. NW, Suite 179
Washington, DC 20016

WFN works to prevent women from appearing to be victims who cannot take responsibility for their behavior. It asserts that the rhetoric of victimization trivializes real abuse, demeans women, and promotes antagonism between the sexes. WFN provides perspectives on family violence, sexual harassment, and other gender-related issues in its quarterly *Women's Freedom Network Newsletter*.

Bibliography

Books

Constance A. Bean	*Women Murdered by the Men They Loved.* Binghamton, NY: Haworth Press, 1992.
Jerry Brinegar	*Breaking Free from Domestic Violence.* Minneapolis: CompCare Publishers, 1992.
Timothy H. Brubaker	*Family Relations: Challenges for the Future.* Newbury Park, CA: Sage Publications, 1993.
Dorothy Ayers Counts, Judith K. Brown, and Jacquelyn C. Campbell	*Sanctions and Sanctuary: Cultural Perspectives on the Beating of Wives.* Boulder, CO: Westview Press, 1992.
Richard J. Gelles and Donileen R. Loseke	*Current Controversies on Family Violence.* Newbury Park, CA: Sage Publications, 1993.
Marsali Hansen and Michele Harway, eds.	*Battering and Family Therapy: A Feminist Perspective.* Newbury Park, CA: Sage Publications, 1993.
N. Zoe Hilton	*Legal Responses to Wife Assault: Current Trends and Evaluation.* Newbury Park, CA: Sage Publications, 1993.
Margareta Hyden	*Woman Battering as Marital Act: The Construction of a Violent Marriage.* Oslo: Scandinavian University Press, 1994.
Scott Johnson	*When "I Love You" Turns Violent.* Far Hills, NJ: New Horizons, 1993.
Ann Jones	*Next Time, She'll Be Dead.* Boston: Beacon Press, 1994.
Ann Jones	*Women Who Kill.* New York: Holt, Rinehart, and Winston, 1980.
Nancy Kilgore	*Every Eighteen Seconds: A Journey Through Domestic Violence.* Volcano, CA: Volcano Press, 1993.
Mary P. Koss et al.	*No Safe Haven: Male Violence, Women at Home, at Work, and in the Community.* Washington, DC: American Psychological Association, 1994.
Elaine J. Leeder	*Treating Abuse in Families.* New York: Springer, 1994.
Donileen R. Loseke	*The Battered Woman and Shelters: The Social Construction of Wife Abuse.* Albany: State University of New York Press, 1992.
Michael Steinman, ed.	*Women Battering: Policy Responses.* Cincinnati: Anderson Publishing Co., 1992.
Larry Tifft	*The Battering of Women: The Failure of Intervention and the Case for Prevention.* Boulder, CO: Westview Press, 1993.

Periodicals

Carol J. Adams — "Help for the Battered," *Christian Century*, June 29–July 6, 1994.

Joseph R. Biden — "Domestic Violence: A Crime, Not a Quarrel," *Trial*, vol. 29, no. 6, June 1993. Available from the Association of Trial Lawyers of America, 1050 31st St. NW, Washington, DC 20007-4499.

Tiffany Devitt and Jennifer Downey — "Battered Women Take a Beating from the Press," *Extra*, special issue, 1992. Available from FAIR, 130 W. 25th St., New York, NY 10001.

Susan Douglas — "Blame It on Battered Women," *Progressive*, August 1994.

Jean Bethke Elshtain — "Battered Reason," *New Republic*, October 5, 1992.

Jean Bethke Elshtain — "Women and the Ideology of Victimization," *World & I*, April 1993.

David Frum — "Women Who Kill," *Forbes*, January 18, 1993.

Nancy Gibbs — "'Til Death Do Us Part," *Time*, January 18, 1993.

Casey G. Gwinn — "Can We Stop Domestic Violence?" *American Jails*, March/April 1995. Available from 2053 Day Rd., Ste. 100, Hagerstown, MD 21740-9795.

Michele Ingrassia and Melinda Beck — "Patterns of Abuse," *Newsweek*, July 4, 1994.

Journal of Contemporary Criminal Justice — Special issue on domestic violence, vol. 10, no. 3, September 1994.

George Lardner Jr. — "How Kristin Died," *Washington Post National Weekly Edition,* January 4–10, 1993. Available from 1150 15th St. NW, Washington, DC 20071.

Wendy McElroy — "The Unfair Sex?" *National Review*, May 1, 1995.

Ms. — Special section on domestic violence, September/October 1994.

Sara Paretsky — "The Hidden War at Home," *New York Times*, July 7, 1994.

Stanton Peele — "Making Excuses: Betrayed Men and Battered Women Get Away with Murder," *National Review*, November 21, 1994.

Jody Raphael — "Domestic Violence and Welfare Reform," *Poverty & Race*, vol. 4, no. 1, January/February 1995. Available from 1711 Connecticut Ave. NW, Ste. 207, Washington, DC 20009.

Elayne Rapping — "What Evil Lurks in the Hearts of Men?" *Progressive*, November 1994.

Donna Shalala — "Domestic Terrorism," *Vital Speeches of the Day*, May 15, 1994.

Jill Smolowe — "When Violence Hits Home," *Time*, July 4, 1994.

Mark Thompson — "The Living Room War," *Time*, May 23, 1994.

Index

Abused Women's Aid in Crisis, 13
Alternative to Violence, 38
American Civil Liberties Union, 78
Antelope Valley Domestic Violence
  Council, 87
Anti-Violence Project, 78
Archives of Internal Medicine, 72
Arthur, Carol, 29, 31, 36, 69
Associated Press, 71

"The Battered Husband Syndrome"
  (Steinmetz), 17, 78, 84
The Battered Woman Syndrome (Walker),
  18
battered women
  characteristics of, 12
  defined, 121
  escape plans for, 25-27
  frequency of abuse, 12, 22, 37, 81
  history of, 10
  psychological abuse, 15
  self-defense for, 17-19
  shelters for, 19
  symptoms/circumstances of battering,
    13-15
    marital rape, 13-14
    and pregnancy, 14
    sexual intimacy, 14-15
    sexual jealousy, 14
  underreporting of occurrence, 11-12
  why they remain with abusive mate,
    16-17
  wife's violence causes beating, 59-60
  see also men who abuse; police, law
  suits against; women
blacks
  and domestic violence, 37-40
Bobbitt, John, 68, 70
Bobbitt, Lorena, 65, 70
Boston Globe, 44
Boyz N the Hood (movie), 38
Browne, A., 54, 55, 56, 57
Bureau of Justice Statistics, 83, 87

California Women's Law Center, 66, 69
Cartier, Michael, 44
Chicago Abused Women Coalition, 25
children
  murdered as result of domestic
    violence, 76, 87
  as reason for leaving abusive mate,
    34-35

as reason for staying with abusive
  mate, 17
Children's Rights Coalition, 84
Christopher, S., 56
clinical fallacy
  in assault reporting, 58
CNN, 73
Commonwealth Fund study, 72
Conflict Tactics Scales (CTS), 51
Conjugal Crime (Davidson), 12
Constantine, Emperor, 10
Cornerstone (Minneapolis), 31
Corpus Christi Women's Shelter, 25
Cose, Ellis, 86
Crime Control Institute, 73
Crossfire (TV program), 71, 80
cycle theory of violence, 17
  breaking the cycle, 19
Cypress Hill (group), 39

date rape, 38-39
DeShaney, Joshua, 46-47
Deshaney, Melody, 46-47
DeShaney, Randy, 46-47
DeShaney decision by Supreme Court,
  46-49
Dobash, Rebecca, 18, 54
Dobash, Russell, 18, 54
Domestic Abuse Awareness Project, 24
Domestic Abuse Project, 29, 69
domestic violence
  both genders cause, 83-85
  and family court, 44
  gender differences in, 51-52
  harms men and women, 65-70
  is problem for black women, 37-40
  is problem for male victims, 50-64
  is problem for professional women,
    28-36
  is serious problem for women, 22-27
  is widespread problem, 10-21
  justice system should take it seriously,
    41-49
  media misreport, 80-82
  problem is exaggerated, 71-57
    for men, 86-88
  psychological abuse as, 15, 32
  stalking as, 76
  women are responsible, 76-79
  see also battered women
Domestic Violence Training Project, 29
Dr. Dre, 39

Dunn, Katherine, 76
Durkin, Tish, 64

escape plans for battered women, 25-27

fallacies, in assault reporting, 58
family court, and domestic violence, 44
Family Violence: Crime and Justice, 28
FBI statistics, 12, 18, 51, 73, 77, 87
fear, and staying with abusive mate, 16
Feld, S.L., 57, 59, 60
Ferrato, Donna, 24
finances, and staying with abusive mate,
  17
Finkelhor, David, 13
Flowers, R. Barri, 10
frequency of abuse
  is often exaggerated, 71-75
  of men, 17-18
  of women, 12, 22, 37
Friedman, Lucy, 38, 40
Frontline (TV program), 41-42

gays. *See* homosexual relationships
Gelles, Richard, 12, 14, 50-53, 57-58, 72,
  77-78, 81
George, Malcolm, 67-69
Getto Boys, 39
Goode, Erica, 22
Gregware, P., 55, 56, 57
guilt, as reason for staying with abusive
  mate, 17

Hart, Barbara, 60, 73
Hill, Anita, 23, 71
Hiraga, Martin, 78
Holmes, Lorraine, 29-32, 34
homosexual relationships
  violence in, 78, 81

Ice Cube, 38-39
Intimate Violence (Straus and Gelles), 81

Johnson, Hillary, 28
Jones, Ann, 41
Journal of Marriage and Families, 84
*Journal of the American Medical
  Association* (JAMA), 73
*Journal for the National Association of
  Social Workers*, 84
Jurik, N. C., 55, 56, 57
justice system
  as abuser's haven, 31-32
  and domestic violence, 41-49
  law suits against police, 23, 45-48

Kantor, G. Kaufman, 54
Kentucky Commission on Women, 52
Kinsley, Michael, 80-81

Kuehl, Sheila James, 66, 69

Lardner, Kristin, 44
law suits, against police, 23, 45-48
legal system. *See* justice system
Leo, John, 80
lesbians. *See* homosexual relationships
Los Angeles Times, 80, 87

McNeeley, R. L., 84
MacNeil/Lehrer NewsHour, 72, 74
marital rape, 13-14
media, misreport domestic violence,
  80-82
Men-Center, 68
men who abuse, 82
  black batterers, 38-39
  characteristics of, 12-13
  reasons for abusing, 15-16
men who are abused, 50-64
  different kinds of attacks, 57-59
  frequency of, 17-18
  leave the relationship, 69
  men's shelter, 87
  often don't tell, 68-69
  problem is exaggerated, 86-88
"Murder in Families" (Bureau of Justice
  Statistics), 83
murder of children, 76, 87
murder of spouses
  comparative homicide rates, 54, 67
  as self-defense, 18-19, 55-57
    frequency of, 18
  by women, 17-19, 87
  of women, 12, 73, 77, 87

National Center for Men, 86
National Coalition Against Domestic
  Violence, 72
National Commission Against Domestic
  Violence, 42
National Crime Panel report, 51
National Crime Survey, 13
National Crime Victimization survey
  (NCVS), 51-53, 72, 77
  1973 to 1992, 66
  1979 to 1987, 13
  1987 to 1991, 11-12, 28-29
National Family Violence survey, 12, 55,
  72, 77, 81, 84
National Gay and Lesbian Task Force, 78
National Institute for Mental Health, 87
National Organization for Women, 75
National Survey of Households and
  Families, 52, 55
Newsweek, 73
The New Victorians (Denfeld), 79
New York Newsday, 80
New York Times, 67

New York University Law Review, 74
Next Time, She'll Be Dead (Jones), 41
Novello, Antonia, 73
NWA (rap group), 39

"One Less Bitch" (song), 39

Pagelow, M. D., 53
Pennsylvania Coalition Against
    Domestic Violence, 73
Penthouse, 67
People magazine, 65
police
    and domestic violence calls, 54
    law suits against, 23, 45-48
    see also justice system
Policing Domestic Violence (Sherman), 73
"A Population-Based Study of Injuries in
    Inner City Women," 73
pregnancy, and abuse, 14
professional women
    domestic violence is problem for, 28-36
Project Protect, 23
psychological abuse, 32
    defined, 15

Race Matters (West), 39, 40
Rainbow Services (Los Angeles), 67, 72
rape, 13-14, 38-39
Rape in Marriage (Russell), 12
rap music, and abuse of women, 38-39
Reno, Janet, 23
representative sample fallacy
    in assault reporting, 58
Riding the Donkey Backwards (George), 67
role expectations, and staying with
    abusive mate, 17
Russell, Diana, 12-14

self-defense for battered women, 17-19
    murder as, 18-19
self-esteem, and abuse, 12
sexual intimacy, and battering, 14-15
sexual jealousy, and battering, 14
shelters
    for battered men, 87
    for battered women, 19
Sherman, Lawrence, 73
Sherven, Judith, 83, 88
"Signs to Look For in a Battering
    Personality" (San Diego P.D.), 24
Simpson, Nicole Brown, 22-23, 31, 76, 86
Simpson, O. J., 22-23, 71, 76, 80, 85-86
Smith, Rita, 72, 73
Sniechowski, James, 83

social stigma, and staying with abusive
    mate, 17
social structure theory
    for male violence, 16
Social Work journal, 84
Sommers, Christina Hoff, 74, 80
stalking, 76
Stark, Evan, 29, 30, 35-36, 59
Steinmetz, Suzanne K., 17, 51, 78, 84
Stets, J. E., 51, 52
Straus, Murray, 12, 50-61, 66-67, 72, 77-
    78, 81
Sullivan, Shawn, 37
Super Bowl hoax (1993), 78

Thurman, Charles, 45
Thurman, Tracey, 45, 46, 47

underreporting of spousal abuse, 11-12
U.S. Department of Justice, 83
U.S. Supreme Court, *DeShaney* decision,
    46-49

victim blaming, 60
*The Victimization and Exploitation of
    Women and Children* (Flowers), 10
Victimology magazine, 78, 84
Victim Services (New York City), 38-39
violence
    cycle theory of, 17
        breaking the cycle, 19
    in homosexual relationships, 78
    by wives leads to wife beating, 59-60
Violence Against Women Act, 75

Walker, Lenore E. A., 11, 13, 14, 17, 53
West, Cornel, 39-40
Who Stole Feminism? (Sommers), 74, 80
wife abuse, history of, 10-11
women
    are responsible for domestic violence,
        76-79, 82
    black, and domestic violence, 37-40
    harassment at workplace by spouses, 32
    see also battered women; murder of
        spouses; professional women; wife
        abuse
"Women and Homicide" (Benedek),
    18-19
Women Who Kill (Jones), 41
workplace, harassment at by spouses, 32

Yllo, K., 13
Young, Cathy, 71